*"Speech is more than words. An effective communicator combines words together with the skill of delivery to produce impact. This includes using voice, eye contact, gestures, and incorporating these into the external environment to produce a message that will be memorable and move the audience to action.*

*Ralph Hillman sets out in clear, understandable language a program—a road map—that will enable the reader to master the skill of delivering dynamic presentations using both voice and body for full impact."*

— *John F. Noonan*, ASP, PRP, CGA, International President 1989–90, Toastmasters International, Toastmasters Accredited Speaker, Formally National Director of Business Training, Business Development Bank of Canada

*"Congratulations on your masterpiece . . . that's the only way I can describe your book. It will take the dedicated professional speaker to the next level of excellence in their careers. It is well researched and contains an incredible amount of valuable information. You are to be commended."*

— *Jos. J. Charbonneau*, CSP, CPAE, Presentations, Inc.

*"Your book,* Delivering Dynamic Presentations: Using Your Voice and Body for Impact, *looks great. It's a must book for all serious communicators. A power packed dynamic book that will aid individuals to improve their communication skills instantly. Our listeners will gain the full impact of what we are saying, if we understand and use the voice and body techniques recommended in this book."*

— *Bennie E. Bough*, International President, 1992–93, Toastmasters International

D0367870

# A word about this series from Toastmasters International

Who needs another book on public speaking, let alone a series of them? After all, this is a skill best learned by practice and "just doing it," you say.

But if practice is the best solution to public speaking excellence, why is this world so full of speakers who can't speak effectively? Consider politicians, business executives, sales professionals, teachers, trainers, clerics, and even "professional" speakers who often fail to reach their audiences because they make elementary mistakes, such as speaking too fast or too long, failing to prepare adequately, and forgetting to consider their audiences.

As we experience in Toastmasters Clubs, practice and feedback are important and play major roles in developing your speaking skills. But insight and tips from people who have already been where you are might help ease some bumps along the road, reinforce some basic public speaking techniques, and provide guidance on handling special speech problems and situations you may encounter. The purpose of *The Essence of Public Speaking Series* is to help you prepare for the unexpected, warn you of the pitfalls, and help you ensure that the message you want to give is indeed the same one the audience hears.

This series features the accumulated wisdom of experts in various speech-related fields. The books are written by trained professionals who have spent decades writing and delivering speeches and training others. The series covers the spectrum of speaking, including writing, using humor, customizing particular topics for various audiences, and incorporating technology into presentations.

Whether you are an inexperienced or seasoned public speaker, *The Essence of Public Speaking Series* belongs on your bookshelf because no matter how good you are, there is always room for improvement. The books are your key to becoming a more effective speaker. Do you have the self-discipline to put into practice the techniques and advice offered in them?

I honestly believe that every person who truly wants to become a confident and eloquent public speaker can become one. Success or failure depends on attitude. There is no such thing as a "hopeless case." If you want to enhance your personal and professional progress, I urge you to become a better public speaker by doing two things:

- Read these books.
- Get on your feet and practice what you've learned.

Terrence J. McCann
*Executive Director, Toastmasters International*

# DELIVERING
# DYNAMIC
# PRESENTATIONS
## Using Your Voice and Body for Impact

### RALPH HILLMAN
*Middle Tennessee State University*

### WILLIAM D. THOMPSON
*Series Editor*

**ALLYN AND BACON**

Boston   London   Toronto   Sydney   Tokyo   Singapore

0-205-26810-2

Printed in the United States of America
10 9 8 7 6 5 4 3 2 1    02 01 00 99 98

# Contents

**PART IV/ Growing in Delivery Skills**

# Foreword

## "YODA HILLMAN":
### A LONG TIME AGO,
#### ON A CAMPUS
##### FAR,
##### FAR
###### AWAY . . .

I was a man of 22 working on my degree at Middle Tennessee State University. People referred to me as happy-go-lucky. That was not entirely true. Something had been stopping me from enjoying each day, and that was my voice. I was confident with the words I was saying, but I was insecure about how they sounded.

I just didn't like the way I sounded. Sometimes my voice would sound good and then two hours later it would sound weak. I tried to improve my voice by making it deeper or louder, but it was not helping. It became bothersome to talk to someone. I would analyze my voice with every word I said. I was so concerned with how I was sounding that I forgot what the conversation was about. I was in Vocal Hell. The temperature was tolerable but the pain was overwhelming! People had no idea what I was going through while I tried to talk to them. I just didn't want to talk anymore. I was so desperate for a stronger voice that I would have settled for one of those electronic voice boxes that heavy smokers who have had their larynx removed need.

I was searching for help to end my vocal nightmare for the next few months. I started to believe that my efforts were futile. I was just about to throw in the towel and live with my voice as it was. But this person appeared who said she would help me. I told her of my problem and asked if there was any logical solution.

She spoke of a man named Hillman, Yoda Hillman. She told me that my answer could be found by Yoda. I was intrigued. Yoda? Really? I found out where Hillman lived and began the journey to meet him. The area around Yoda's home was muddy, some might say swampy. I then passed the rough terrain and made my way to the second floor of the speech and theatre building, BDA. Something felt right about this place.

I saw someone and asked him if he knew of Yoda. The man answered, "Of course I know Yoda; he lives in that room." The man laughed at me and continued on his path. I walked across the hall and saw a room that was obviously occupied. I went inside and was face-to-neck with a tall man. I was expecting a short green voice expert, but he wasn't green, and short didn't describe him either. Since he was prestigious and wise, I was a little nervous about talking to Yoda. I opened up my mouth and tried to tell him my problem. He knew right away why I had come to him. When he spoke to me, I realized that his voice had been mastered.

I was amazed with the clarity of his voice. He explained to me the problems causing my weak voice. What I had was a vocal condition known as breathiness. But I had other problems, too. My posture was also limiting the sound of my voice. I asked him if I could change my weak voice and I was relieved to hear him answer, "Of course you can." He told me of the VOICE and how I could learn the ways of it. I was very interested.

He decided to take me under his wing and teach me what he knew. He began fundamental VOICE training. Since he was bigger than I expected, I decided that he wouldn't ride in my backpack. I had to have the knowledge in my mind. He began to challenge the use of my voice to see what he had to work with. Essentially, he was making me confront my fears in front of him. I struggled to fight off my old breathy voice with the new techniques I was being given. I was making progress and Yoda looked pleased. Yoda told me that the change would stay for a while, but I would have to keep visiting him so the new sound would be maintained. He told me that one day I would know the ways of the VOICE.

Yoda suggested that I enroll in his class, Yoda VOICE. I knew I had to spend time with him and learn the ways of the VOICE. What better way to do that than to take a class with him! After I took his class, I was very satisfied with my voice; it sounded very strong. I received many compliments on it. My vocal hell became vocal heaven. After achieving the VOICE, my life changed drastically. I was happier than ever and I also met a woman who has changed my life!

Even though my voice will try to go back to the old breathy, weak voice on occasion, I am still able to overcome that when I hear Yoda's voice say, "Derek, use the VOICE."

"Yoda Hillman" by Derek Hanson
(Used with permission)

# Preface

## BELIEF, TRUST, AND CREDIBILITY

This is a book about communication choices. Found within these chapters are the delivery behaviors that will help you to look, sound, and feel better as a speaker. We will assume that you have content that you believe is worthy of sharing and that you sincerely want to share it with audiences. We are not going to deal with its organization or the research strategies used to give it form. We are going to deal with the delivery of your content, your voice, your face, your body, your appearance . . . the whole package.

It is important to realize that how you visually and audibly present yourself has an even stronger impact than it ever has before. Becoming aware of all those variables that can impact the perceptions of an audience will be our goal. But on the front end, you must know this: There is a dramatic difference between liking someone and trusting someone. The breathy speaker serves as the best evidence.

Most of us know someone who is very likable and who is also very soft-spoken and breathy; he or she uses a lot of air when speaking. Along comes a task or project requiring leadership, wise use of funds, and allocation of personal resources. Do we even consider our breathy speaker as a candidate for this role? Very likely not. We perceive our breathy speaker to be too weak to meet the expectations of the position. We don't trust that our friend will make wise decisions, even through we know he or she would try. Even though we like this breathy speaker, we don't consider him or her to be credible with the folks he or she would have to interact with. This situation provides us with a real dilemma because of the incongruence that is created between our personal and professional feelings.

For those of us who use certain vocal behaviors habitually, such as breathiness, we don't want to create this dilemma in the feelings of friends, coworkers, and, most important, audiences. What can we do to avoid this dilemma? We can examine our communication patterns, change those that are hindering us, and work to develop new, more effective methods of communicating. That is the goal of this book on delivery.

To achieve this goal, we will first take a look at the relationship between content, delivery, audiences, and the speaker. How does a speaker's content impact an audience depending on its delivery? Once we examine this relationship, we will discuss making changes in how we deliver our content and what is involved in making those changes. The first and most important things for us to look at concerning this idea are learning patterns and how we can transform old, undesirable habits into new, more desired patterns of behavior.

In the next part, we will begin examining the audible elements of delivery. We will discuss voice qualities. How do we sound to ourselves and others? What qualities do our voices have that also relay ideas to others about who we are as individuals? We will look at the 10 voice qualities and the stereotypes that are associated with them. In our culture, stereotypes are inevitable, so we'll discuss how we can change our sound as well as the perception others have of us.

Then we'll go through other components of delivery, such as rate, pitch, and volume. There will be exercises to help achieve a desired rate of speaking, a pleasing variety of pitch, and sufficient volume when speaking. These components of delivery are usually known about by speakers, but what may not be known is the most effective way to use them. Once we master these, we'll move on to the importance of using "The Big Three." Using "The Big Three" will give us posture that will be more visibly satisfying to our audiences and will reduce the amount of tension we have in our neck and shoulder muscles, which allows us to sound better and to improve our self-concepts. We will have sufficient breath support to give us clear, abundant speech. Exercises in how to do cleansing breaths to "rejuvenate" our breathing patterns will also be discussed. We'll learn how to breathe to get more oxygen into our bodies and to our brains.

Then we will become educated on the anatomy of the vocal process. When we discuss our voices, the voice qualities, and how to produce them, we need to know what is going on inside our bodies. We will look at the physical structure and the responsibilities these structures have in helping us to produce speech and to be effective speakers.

Finally in the second part, we will discuss articulation, enunciation, and pronunciation. We will look at how to correct mistakes we may make when producing certain words. We'll learn the International Phonetic Alphabet to help us discriminate sounds and to produce the words of our language correctly.

In the third part, we will examine the visible elements in delivery for speakers. We will first look at the speaker's body as a whole and the visual appearance that is seen by audiences. How should speakers dress and how should we move while on stage? What are the best gestures to use while speaking? What gestures are distracting? And what about eye contact? What is the best way to keep eye contact with audiences? These components all work together in helping an audience form lasting opinions about a speaker.

Next, we look at the external factors that assist in effective presentations. How do we adjust to certain room settings so that we can be seen and heard by all audience members? Visual aids are always vital in helping audiences understand our message. We will look at effective ways to use visual aids to our advantage. Finally, what do we need to do so that the public address systems we use will enhance our delivery instead of detracting from it?

The last part concerns how we can continually maintain and develop delivery skills. We will discuss ways to keep our bodies and our voices healthy. To make sure that we keep our delivery skills sharp, the best thing to do is to consistently tape (whether it be audio or video) ourselves and then critique what we hear and see. We will review what to look for and what questions to ask when we do our regular critiques. We'll also talk about other ways of becoming (and staying!) skilled speakers, such as utilizing public speaking courses, workshops, Toastmasters, the National Speakers Association, and voice coaches.

# ACKNOWLEDGMENTS

All of this is a gift from God, and I am very grateful for the experience and the opportunity.

None of my professional activity, as a teacher, speaker, consultant, or writer would be possible were it not for my beautiful bride of almost 35 years and the cooperative attitudes of my children.

My mother got me started speaking, pretty much against my will, when I was 14 years old in 1952. Looking at me—I was well over six feet tall with a bad case of hay fever and had just survived a 30-foot fall that would give me back pain for the rest of my life—she did not think farming was my best career option. She said to me, "As a minister, doctor, or lawyer, you will be doing a lot of speaking." Her view was to start immediately. So I did. Those early speaking opportunities launched my professional speaking career. I did not know I was a professional back then. None of us thought of ourselves as professional speakers. We just gave speeches and were often paid for our efforts.

Many thanks to:

■ Dr. Hugh Seabury, at the State University of Iowa, Speech and Dramatic Arts Department, my first advisor.

Dr. Paul Heinberg, SUI, taught me what he knew about his specialty, Voice and Diction. We authored *Communication Strategies* together (self-published).

Delorah Jewel, who coauthored *Work for Your Voice*, a text used in Voice and Diction classes at MTSU.

■ Marie Przybyski, Bill Conger, Melody Hilty, Becky Jordan, and Lara James actually worked for me in my office at MTSU. As office managers, they freed me up to concentrate on learning more about speaking and credible delivery. Becky came back for the last few months of manuscript preparation. Her organizational skills were invaluable.

■ Buddy, Joe, Jay, Gale (our first group), Charlie (my prayer partner), Jack, Jeff, Mac, Dave, Bob, and John (our current group), who have all been members of a men's accountability group that has been meeting weekly at 6:00 A.M. on Fridays for over 8 years.

The Tennessee Speakers Association of the National Speakers Association broadened my perspective of professional speaking.

Sonny Reynolds, Pat Prosser, the Toastmasters clubs of Tennessee, Irma Perry, and Toastmasters International all helped me to achieve a long-held communication goal, being a keynote speaker at a Toastmasters International Convention. The dream became a reality in Toronto, Canada, in 1993.

■ All those students and clients who allowed me to work with them on the most intimate part of their lives, their communication delivery patterns. They provided me with a wealth of significant learning opportunities.

# CONTENT, DELIVERY, AUDIENCES, AND THE SPEAKER

## What You Say and How You Say It

It's not what you say, it's how you say it that counts. I believe that statement to be true when the following assumptions are realities: The speaker does have something to say which is well organized and supported and the speaker is sincere in desiring to share this information with the audience.

If these two assumptions are realities, how the message is delivered will be a determining factor in audience enjoyment, understanding, and acceptance. If the delivery is smooth, the speech will likely be a success. If the speech is delivered poorly, the chances of it being rated as successful are diminished dramatically. The poor delivery scenario is particularly sad when the speaker really is sincere in desiring to share information. As audience members, we are sad because the speaker has our empathy and we are disappointed if the speaker is not interesting.

We all love experiencing speakers who deliver good content well. We get very frustrated when good content is delivered poorly. We want to participate in the content and don't want to be distracted by poor delivery.

But what about those speakers who, we perceive, have no content? If their delivery is "smooth" and relatively distraction-free, regardless of the quality of the content, we will likely listen and eagerly accept the opportunity to learn.

When we force the issue and ask whether they value content or delivery potential more, audiences will indicate that they came to hear good content. They are using their intellects to answer. But put these same people in the real role of audience members and their behavior almost always reveals the opposite response. Audience members are not likely to sit through a poorly delivered speech, regardless of the content's quality. They comment upon exiting the room (often during the speech!), "Good content, just not very interesting." When audience members say, "Interesting," they are usually referring to the quality of the delivery.

If these audience members are also subjected to some great delivery of speeches containing little content, they are more apt to wait the speaker out, and, when leaving, to say, "It was OK." Some will comment as they are leaving, "But the speaker didn't say anything."

At conventions where there are equally content-rich concurrent sessions, potential audience members will "test the waters" to check on delivery variables before committing to listen to the whole thing. They simply do not want to be disappointed in the delivery. They "did not come to this convention to be bored." Audience members do not want to be distracted from the content by poor delivery.

As audience members, we do have a choice. Increasing numbers of audience members are making these choices known by where they spend their money. Seminar companies offer learning opportunities concerning the same information that can be acquired from books or from training sessions offered by various companies. But these seminar companies are successful because they deliver good content and the presentation is delivered well. If the content was not delivered well, the company would fail.

Professional speakers must supply audio- and/or videotapes, often of their whole presentations, to meeting planners so that they can make a choice among the many speakers available. Most speakers in any content area are covering the same basic material. Although meeting planners always check for quality of material, their biggest concern is the quality of the speaker's delivery. They often ask, "Do they look good?" "Do they sound good?" and "Will this speaker put my audience members to sleep or keep them interested?"

We all know people who are experts, and we recognize that they know their content well. We just don't want to hear them talk about it. But we also know speakers who are experts whom we have heard before and are eager to hear again. It's because of how they deliver their messages. How many of us have speakers on tape that we listen to over and over again? Why don't we choose to listen to other speakers delivering the same content?

For most of us, content and delivery do not make up an either/or discussion. We want both. We want good content delivered well.

If we look beyond the concept of content, we might be able to understand the delivery concern better. I believe the problem lies in the weakness of words as instruments of communication. Words are powerful, but they are also abstract. Words represent thoughts, patterns, processes, and concepts. But words are not the thoughts, patterns, processes, and concepts they represent. The words are one level of abstraction away from the real things. To get an audience to understand words, a speaker must get the audience to translate those words into the same (or similar) mental images the speaker is using. This process is difficult and can be very confusing. Granted, selecting the appropriate words is essential for the speaker. But how these words are delivered will determine if the building of a similar mental image in the minds of the audience is successful. This book addresses most of the options available to speakers allowing them to be proficient at creating mental images in the minds of their audiences.

In our culture, if the meaning of a speaker's words is inconsistent or incongruent with that speaker's body language and tonality, we will choose to believe the body language and tonality rather than the words. The words have to be there; they are important. But how the words are delivered will impact the message communicated more than will the meaning of the words themselves.

Speakers who deliver content that is well organized, and who also exhibit a burning desire to share that information, will be most successful if they use their voices and bodies consistently with the meanings of the words they are sharing. How true that statement is will depend greatly on the makeup of the audience. Are audience members right-brained or left-brained? Are they cerebral or limbic thinkers? Do they take notes or just prefer to listen and experience the essence of the communication? Are they searching for information or entertainment?

The biggest audience variable can be found by examining audience members' expectations. People don't mind if speakers at an academic subject matter convention, where research findings are most important, read their papers without humor or effective delivery strategies. That would not be true at a Toastmasters International Convention or a National Speakers Association Convention. Much of the power of ideas is diluted or lost when poor body and vocal elements contradict those ideas being put forth by a speaker. The speaker's likability suffers, too.

# 2 LEARNING PATTERNS

## Making Controllable Changes

As stated previously, this book is primarily about communication delivery choices. Most of us recognize that we need to make some choices then work to make them permanent. In order to achieve that permanency, changing some of our current communication behaviors becomes mandatory. For most of us, change is difficult. We are reluctant even to attempt it because we are often afraid of the whole idea of change. Breaking the whole change concept down into smaller pieces might make it easier to swallow and digest, especially when we realize that changing can make us better communicators.

Let me go through a change process with you. We will call this change process the feedback loop. We will be looking at behaviors already in place within ourselves, our feedforward system. Since we want to alter what is already in progress, we have to look back at it, hence, the feedback loop. I know it's not very original. It's been used before. But it is very helpful in describing what is going on as we get involved in the change process. This feedback loop will allow us to **inspect** the behavior we desire to "change." Then we need to **compare** that old, undesirable behavior with a more acceptable, desired behavior and work at **correcting,** or practicing the new behavior. We practice this new behavior until it becomes our preference or habitual behavior, **precorrection**.

First, though, let's deal with some models that will make this discussion easier to understand by disclosing what is going on behind the scenes (actually up in our brain). Each of us has a number of habits or behaviors that we perform without thinking about the specifics of performing them. They happen seemingly automatically. When the appropriate stimulus occurs, we exhibit the behavior pretty much the same way each time. Each of these behaviors or behavior patterns is the reaction of our body to commands from a series of connections in our brains. Once that series of connections is stimulated, the brain sends command messages to the parts of our body necessary to execute the behavior(s). We are not aware of any of this activity at the conscious level. We don't need to even think about the step-by-step detail of the behavior we are doing. We just do the behavior, seemingly, automatically. Habits are like that. Again, we call this collection of habits our feedforward system.

Before we go on to cover the rest of the feedback loop, let's look at the automatic nature of our habits. To demonstrate the automatic nature of these behaviors (habits), as well as the subconscious nature of their performance, let's specify some examples. The difficult-to-learn but long-remembered patterns of behavior are numerous. For example, tying your shoes, buttoning a shirt, brushing your teeth, and dressing yourself are perfect examples of feedforward patterns. But there are some communication behaviors that are much more subtle but equally as long remembered. I would like you to recall a time when you felt you were being imposed on in a relationship. As you expressed your feelings of powerlessness to change the situation, how did you verbalize this? Do you use the nasal (through the nose), breathy (using lots of air), and often thin (high-pitched) sound of your voice?

Many people have a tendency to do this. It's often expressed in a stressed-out, grunt-like "uh."

You must do this behavior aloud to sense the experience of it. Remember to use the breathy, nasal, and thin voice qualities as you say, "Ooooh!" while continuing to come up in pitch. It is really a whine of frustration. If you have never done this pattern before, think of those people whom you have heard use it.

My favorite feedforward pattern experience happened a couple of years ago. It is not a speech example, but it is such a clear example of the strength of our feedforward systems. I'm usually up at 5:00 A.M., and by 5:30, I'm on the street doing my three mile walk. I come home and hit the shower. I then get dressed and head out. It's a seven-day-a-week routine. On this particular day, when I got to the parking lot at work, I was surprised to find it empty. It was Sunday, I realized. I had dressed for church and actually looked at the Sunday paper before leaving the house. Once I got in the car, though, I apparently switched on the feedforward system. My feedforward system is programmed to go directly to the work site. It was as if the car just took off by itself. I did not turn off the automatic pilot process until I got to the empty parking lot. Has your feedforward system ever taken you on a similar trip?

Our habits are so automatic that we need a very structured system to understand the process enough to implement a change. The structured system for implementing a change is called the *feedback loop*. The four steps of the feedback loop are inspection, comparison, correction, and precorrection. Before we continue, let's use an example of a speech behavior that we might desire to change. Like most Americans, I tend to use a breathy voice quality when I speak, particularly in a relaxed atmosphere. Too often, the breathy sound is accompanied by a "couch potato" posture with poor breath support. Often, other people in the room find it difficult to understand what I'm saying. Although I am not consciously aware that I am doing it, others notice it and call the weak sound and look to my attention. I have even been known to deny that I am doing it. I simply don't hear it, although I do "feel it" on the inside.

How can I change that behavior? First, I need to recognize intellectually that I have the inappropriately breathy sound, the poor posture, the shallow breathing, and the weak voice. I must feel it, hear it, and be aware of it to the point that I am bothered by all of it. This is the **inspection** phase of the change process.

A lot of us never recognize or acknowledge that we have a behavior that needs modification. We utilize all the avoidance behavior we can muster. Until we "own up" to the behavior, the rest of the change process will never happen. We have to, at least intellectually, acknowledge that we do the behavior and that we have other choices of behavior available. It's at this point that we can best use the services of a good delivery coach. To move from intellectual recognition to actually sensing the behaviors as we execute them, we need encouragement and help. That help will come when the coach can mimic back the behavior we are exhibiting and also demonstrate the desired behavior.

Playback on audio- and videotape allows us to hear and see ourselves as others do. With someone we trust guiding the way and perhaps even pushing a little, we can openly acknowledge that this set of behaviors needs to be altered. Then we have to practice the new, desired behavior in contrast with the old one to continue to experience the difference.

For years, I used to think that if individuals could recognize and inspect their own behaviors, they could automatically discern and implement the changes that needed to be made. I have come to realize that for the majority of people, that simply will not happen. Even with highly motivated speakers—who want to sound better, who recognize they have distracting behaviors, and who are aware of the possible vocal variable changes—it rarely happens. Speakers are not likely to participate in negative practice routines comparing their problem behaviors with the desired behaviors in order to experience the differences on their own. They need a voice coach guiding them.

The change process begins with the *inspection* step. But it will not continue until we participate actively in comparison/contrast exercises (the *comparison* step). We must learn to be free enough of both the old and the new behaviors that we can turn them on and off at the conscious level. When we become sick of our distracting behaviors and realize that we have more preferable choices available, change is possible. Until that sick-of-it moment occurs, the current habits will stay. We will probably need someone—a good coach—guiding us, maybe even pushing us, to make changes and to be persistent and consistent in producing those changes.

To understand the importance of the *comparison* step, consider the brain activity and resultant behavior patterns that are already at work. Once a stimulus occurs, the brain jumps into action to initiate the only pattern of behavior it knows. If we are going to have our brains set off a different behavior pattern more consistent with our desires, we must interrupt that first message headed to those cell connections in our brains and tell our brains to generate this new behavior, often in elaborate, step-by-step detail. Not surprisingly, it takes our brains longer to initiate and complete the new behavior than the old one.

It is very hard to stop the old chain of events and insert the new one. The best way is to consciously practice doing both behaviors back to back (see Figure 2.1). You need to repeat this exercise until you are confident that you can

**Figure 2.1**

# Old Habit/New Habit

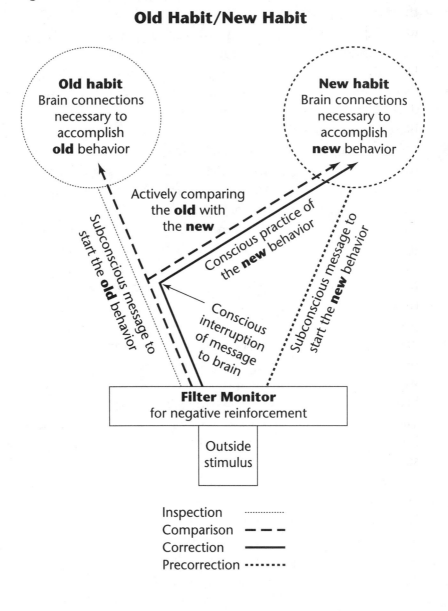

**Old habit**
Brain connections
necessary to
accomplish
**old** behavior

**New habit**
Brain connections
necessary to
accomplish
**new** behavior

Actively comparing
the **old** with
the **new**

Conscious practice of
the **new** behavior

Subconscious message to
start the **old** behavior

Subconscious message to
start the **new** behavior

Conscious
interruption
of message
to brain

**Filter Monitor**
for negative reinforcement

Outside
stimulus

| | |
|---|---|
| Inspection | ·············· |
| Comparison | – – – |
| Correction | ——— |
| Precorrection | ········ |

control turning both behaviors off and on at will. You will
then be well on the way to acquiring the new desired behavior. You will also be sick of the old behavior!

Now it's time to turn on the new behavior all the time.
Do the *correction* step. Very consciously practice using the
new behavior everywhere appropriate. Make sure you are
doing it the way you want it done when it has become a
habit. Practice does not make perfect, but perfect practice
does. This step can take minutes to months, depending on
the person, the behavior, and the amount of practice time
devoted to it.

If you practice consistently, a situation will soon arise in
which your new behavior is called for. In my case, it was one
of those family discussions. I wasn't thinking about behaving
in any certain way. In fact, I was concentrating on the flow of
the conversation. But out comes the new behavior anyway.
(In my case, the breathiness was not there!) And it came out
just like I had practiced it. I didn't plan it; the new behavior
just happened. It occurred at the subconscious level. This new
behavior pattern is now part of my habit system, my feedforward system. My brain has now chosen to use this new
behavior as the primary pattern of choice. *Precorrection* has
taken place. Using good posture, even at home while relaxing, is now a habit. And when I am called on to speak, the
sound is loud and clear.

So, you have successfully completed your change process
and can happily walk off into the sunset. End of story, right?
Unfortunately not. You may have some surprises coming.
Most of us believe that once we change to a new habit pattern, the old habit is gone, not only from our behavior patterns but also from our brains. The first surprise is that old
habit patterns do not go away; they stay in our brains forever.
We can, with reinforced repetition, convince our brains to use
new habit patterns instead of old ones most of the time. But

sooner or later, our brains will, apparently quite randomly, try out the old behaviors again. The second surprise is that our brains do not have consciences. They don't care which pattern they use in response to a stimulus. Our brains are much like computers; they do what we tell them to do, but we must be careful to monitor the output.

If your brain has several behavior patterns stored and has consistently used just one pattern over a period of time, it will, quite out of the blue, eventually present one of the other patterns. Now, as a speaker, you have a choice; you can stay with this different pattern (the inappropriate one) your brain has just presented, or you can consciously get your brain to continue to generate the pattern you desire.

So we need to add a filter to our model of the brain to illustrate this decision point. It appears after the stimuli and before the brain patterns. The filter's role is to constantly monitor to make sure that the behavior about to be performed is consistent with the speaker's desires. This is necessary because if the brain is allowed to choose an undesirable behavior, that behavior will become, at least for a while, the behavior of choice. As far as the brain is concerned, this undesirable behavior has been reinforced by repetition and will receive preference for a while just because it has been executed. Ask a recovering alcoholic if his or her brain has ever presented the "go ahead, have a drink" option to him or her. Can he or she have just one drink (the old pattern)? Most often, the answer is no. If you step back into an old brain connection, reinforcing the connection by executing the behavior just once, the recovery process must usually begin all over again.

We have been talking about **negative practice**, doing the old, undesirable behavior and then contrasting it with the new, desired behavior until it can be turned on and off as desired. Now it is time for **negative reinforcement**. This process is done by making minor adjustments in our behavior so that we can get back on track. We are able to do this without going back through the feedback loop and to alter the brain connection we are using to generate the desired behavior.

Negative reinforcement can be broken down into two different steps. First, monitor your current behavior so that you realize you are not on track. The second step is actually to make the minor changes needed to get the current behavior on track. For example, when driving a car, we check to see if we are staying in the center of the lane. If not, we begin moving the steering wheel to the right and left as we position the car near the center of the lane. If we do not move the steering wheel, the car will bear to either the right or the left, depending on the driving surface. The car will eventually be positioned out of the desired lane. Making minor adjustments keeps us from getting far off track and we don't have to go through the whole feedback loop again.

I use the negative reinforcement process to keep myself mindful of my shoulders slumping forward. Because I am monitoring my posture, I can make the corrections required to pull my shoulders back and down. If the people I am talking to are having trouble understanding me, I don't need to get angry at them. Because I am monitoring how I sound, I can use the negative reinforcement process to remind me to move my lips more or to decrease my breathiness. Minor changes in my communication behaviors allow me to be effective and efficient as a communicator . . . because I do have choices about how I move and sound, how I deliver.

Figure 2.2 illustrates the idea that when we do shift our communication behaviors, we can change the way our audiences relate to us.

**Figure 2.2**

# A Model for Achieving Communication Change:
## Process for Altering Communication Stereotypes

Any use of a habitual personal communication behavior (Step 1) generates a subconscious internal reaction (Step 4) and a personal response (Step 5), which will be perceived by others (Step 6) with some varying degrees of belief, trust, and credibility.

| Step 1 | Step 2 | Step 3 | Step 4 | Step 5 | Step 6 |
|---|---|---|---|---|---|
| Any use of a habitual personal communication behavior | When confronted with a new situation | Will draw only on past experience | Generating a subconscious internal reaction | And a personal response | Which will be perceived by others with some varying degrees of: |

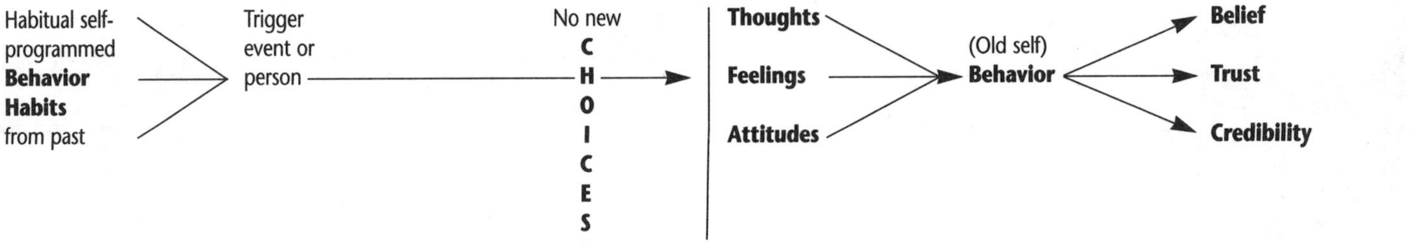

By inspection of your habitual personal communication behaviors (Step 1) when confronted with a "new" trigger event or person (Step 2), you can observe your internal reactions (Step 4) and the resulting communication behaviors (Step 5). The perception of others (Step 6) regarding belief, trust, and credibility in and about you may not be as desired. If, after your inspection (Steps 1, 2), you make the desired communication behavior choice changes (Step 3) your internal reactions (Step 5), your behavior (Step 4), and the audience response (Step 6) will ultimately be improved.

| Step 1 | Step 2 | Step 3 | Step 4 | Step 5 | Step 6 |
|---|---|---|---|---|---|
| Any use of a habitual personal communication behavior | When confronted with a new situation | Will draw only on past experience | Generating a subconscious internal reaction | And a personal response | Which will be perceived by others with some varying degrees of: |

**Trigger**

**Behavior** event

or

**Habits** person

from past

Habitual self-programmed

**C** Posture
**H** Breath support
**O** Neck/shoulder
**I** Voice qualities
**C** Pitch
**E** Rate
**S** Volume

**Thoughts**

**Feelings**

**Attitudes**

(Potential self)

**Behavior**

**Belief**

**Trust**

**Credibility**

# 3 SO YOU WANT TO STUDY YOUR VOICE?

There are many factors that tell us and the world who we are as communicators, whether those factors are accurate or not. These factors include the content of our messages, the sound of our voices, and our physical appearance as seen by others, such as our posture, our basic movements, and our eye contact with audiences. The overall presentation of ourselves as communicators is important. However, the one factor that surfaces as the most important when people make decisions based on their perceptions about who we really are is the sounds of our voices.

The sounds of our voices often help others determine who they think we are and what kind of personalities we may possess. Once that determination of perceptions has been made, the damage is done . . . our first impressions are over. And it takes only a few seconds! Whether we want to admit it or not, the sounds of our voices let the world in on a great deal of information about us. All too often, that perceived information is inconsistent with who we really are on the inside or who we want the world to see. Choices we made earlier in our lives, sometimes without knowing we had other options, have dictated how we sound now.

Becoming aware of the options available to us as speakers allows us to see that we may be able to change how we sound. Once we become aware of how we sound and realize the options available to us, the motivation to change may develop. What is holding us back from delivering a totally new sound is the prospect of actually doing something about it. Most of us will need considerable guided practice to hear a more desired sound or even to recognize the undesirability of the sound we now produce. Knowledge (the content of this book), motivation (our desire to modify how we sound), and practice (over time, often with a professional voice coach) are the three big factors in altering how we sound. Change is hard to deal with, especially when the change must come from our behaviors AND when our behaviors are so much a part of who we perceive ourselves to be.

How many of us have tried saying something differently from the way we normally do or have tried using a different "voice"? Did we feel embarrassed or out of place? Did we feel we were being fake? How many of us worried that our families and friends wouldn't recognize us if we changed how we sound? Did we worry that we would be seen as foolish or odd? These are great defensive, avoidance behavior patterns. We have to put all these concerns behind us if we really believe that changing how we sound will have communication advantages for us.

Sometimes, the painful truth is that most people will be relieved if we don't sound like we normally do! However, they may not notice that we sound different at the conscious level. Rather, they may notice an increase in energy level or an attitude shift. We generally aren't aware of the reason for our perception of people. We just know that our perception may shift slightly. Changing the way we sound can greatly impact ourselves and our speaking careers. Each of us needs to be free to test this for ourselves. Use a voice quality different from the one you use on a regular basis. See if you get different reactions from people you encounter. We must keep in mind that many communication behaviors really control us and may, in fact, inhibit our opportunities. We have to remember that we have the power to control these inhibiting behaviors.

We need to separate who we are (or who we think we are) from our communication behaviors. This is a tougher task than you might think. When people are told that they are very breathy when they talk, they become defensive because they think they are being personally attacked. This is a comment only about a communication behavior, not a comment on the individual's personality or inner self. Most people react in this way; they believe that who they are and their communication behaviors are the same.

If we are going to change our attitudes and behaviors, we must begin looking at our speech behaviors as learned habits that we can modify without directly affecting who we are on the inside. Once we realize that our perception of ourselves and our communication behaviors are separate, we can stop relying on our self-preservation strategies enough to stop defending our inappropriate communication behaviors.

Whether on the platform, on the phone, or face-to-face, we know that first impressions greatly impact the success of our communications with others. Many people we converse with will use that first impression to gauge the remainder of their time with us, from a few seconds to the rest of our lives. Are those first impressions our voices make on others that powerful? Each of us can experience the impact of first impressions by becoming aware of our own responses to the voices of people we do not know very well. We create ideas about people we have just heard for the first time.

Even though we may not "know" anything about the person behind that voice, our brains quickly recall data about people with similar sounding voices we have heard before. Our brain takes that recalled data (traits, characteristics, etc.) and applies it to the owner of this new voice. Within a few seconds, we react to that previously collected data. Whether this data application is accurate in terms of the real person we are addressing appears to be unimportant. In our minds, we already "know" them. In a sense, we have judged them before we have found out "the rest of the story."

This judgment process, regardless of how clumsily or how accurately it is used, is part of our brain's need to categorize and label incoming data. The brain is making a perception decision. We are stereotyping other people on the basis of how others sound to us (we will discuss more about stereotyping in the next chapter). But we operate unaware that how we sound is the primary source of data others use to make their decisions about who we are. We also resist the reality that each of us can change how we sound (if we choose). We have the power to change how people react to us. But we may need help in making the change.

This section of the book is about those options we have about how we sound. We must realize that we have communication choices. We can change vocal behaviors, our postures, our appearances, and our basic movements as communicators. There are other choices we make to allow us to become better communicators. Once we become aware of our options, we can make personal, deliberate decisions about how we sound. We can control our sound instead of allowing our sound to control us.

When we speak, there are certain characteristics, or qualities, that our voices may have. They may be perceived as high-pitched, rather loud, or somewhat dull. Modifying certain characteristics of our voices can create new voice qualities and thus change how we are perceived. Let's begin the process by listing the 10 voice qualities in a quick overview:

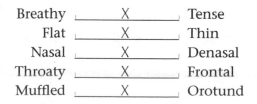

| Breathy | X | Tense |
| Flat | X | Thin |
| Nasal | X | Denasal |
| Throaty | X | Frontal |
| Muffled | X | Orotund |

I have listed the voice qualities in bipolar form. Each pair represents two extremes, or opposites, in how a voice sounds and how it is produced. The bottom four voice quality pairs cannot be produced at the same time by a "normal" person. Only breathy and tense, the first pair of voice qualities in the list, can be performed together. In the upcoming chapters, we'll discuss how the voice qualities sound, how to produce them, and the stereotypes that are associated with them.

Once we study these voice qualities, what can we do with this knowledge? Once we identify the voice quality (or voice qualities) we may have, we can determine if we want to change that sound and the impression or perception our voices give to others. We can then work to diminish that voice quality and to create a more desirable sound for our voices.

The goal in this whole discussion of voice qualities is to get speakers to use the good voice quality habitually. In our list of voice qualities, the $X$ down the middle represents the good voice quality. For a single pair of voice qualities, such as breathy and tense, using good voice quality is producing a sound that is neither too breathy or too tense. This sound is our goal. That area in the middle of each continuum is where none of the voice qualities are apparent and, therefore, distracting. With all 10 qualities, while exaggerating one of the voice qualities, we are automatically diminishing its mate. As you read the description of each pair of voice qualities, keep in mind that getting rid of one means moving toward acquiring the other. The various voice qualities are useful and necessary for emphasis and variety, but work to use good voice quality habitually.

If we are going to study our voices, we must look at some standard considerations regarding our general physical health. Since our health has an effect on our voices and speech production, most people need to heed these considerations before starting voice training. Doing so will help you make sure that your body is healthy and ready for you to speak effectively.

To have healthy voices, we must have healthy bodies. This means eating right and drinking plenty of water. A regular exercise routine keeps us strong and energetic. Making sure we get adequate sleep and giving our bodies sufficient rest is imperative for keeping good health. Furthermore, as speakers, there are certain precautions we need to take to protect our voices. Before speaking, we should avoid certain foods and be sure to keep our throats and vocal folds moisturized. And last, but not least, we need to maintain good mental health by keeping a positive focus throughout the day. These considerations will be discussed in detail in the final section.

It is important for me to point out here that any physical limitations that you may have could dramatically affect how you are able to use the exercises in this book. Even without physical limitations or vocal limitations, some of the exercises may not work for you. Please feel free to contact me to see if there are specific solutions available that may not be covered in this text.

# 4 PERCEPTIONS AND STEREOTYPES

## Could This Be Dialect Reduction?

Perception, according to Webster, is defined as using the senses to become aware and to make judgments. Stereotype is defined as " . . . a conventional notion . . . of a person or group . . . held by a number of people and allowing for no individuality." We use our perceptions and our cultural stereotypes as a filtering system to make judgments about who other people are and what our relationship with them will be. In our culture, lots of different data points are used to give us the sense data for our perceptions of who other people are. We make the initial perception very quickly, generally in seconds. Only time can allow us to validate our perceptions. Size, shape, body movements, clothing, hair, makeup, cars, socioeconomic status, and gestures all add to our information base.

But most of these pale in comparison to the validity we give to the initial sound, the first hearing, of someone's voice. In thinking about perceptions and stereotypes, it is important to remember a few ideas. We are always collecting sense data about people. This includes how they look, how they smell, what they are wearing, and so on. All these sense data points help us identify the initial stereotype we are going to attach to this person we just encountered. We must remember that we get our lasting first impression data from the sound of others' voices and, as a result, voice variables are the biggest contributors to cultural stereotypes.

How many of us have gone to a social gathering and made eye contact with a person across the room? This person "looks" good, exceeding our visual expectations. The clothes are right. The hair is perfect. The movement of the hands, the way this person looks about the room, and the posture are all on target. As we get closer, this person says something quite neutral like, "Hi, how are you?" Because we perceive the sound of this person's voice as high-pitched and nasal, which we have stereotyped as "whining," we choose to direct our attention elsewhere. The physical image data is now challenged in our heads. The sound data takes precedence and we soon find that the person did not even meet our minimum standards or expectations. Regardless of the offensive voice qualities used, how many of us have had similar situations happen to us, many times?

The sound of our voices is ultimately used more than any other variable to determine how others will react to us. We use this perception data to generate stereotypes. After listening to someone with a high-pitched, nasal voice, we determine that they are whining. We will automatically make this judgment call on anyone else we encounter speaking with this same sound.

The comforting thing about this scenario is that most of the time we are correct. The characteristics of the new person do match up with the previously noted criteria. The tragedy of this scenario is that once in a while, the personality of the new voice does not match up but, because of our initial responses, we are rarely likely to find out. Those first impressions make such an impact that we generally do not bother to look past the voice to check or validate the stereotype we imposed on the new person.

Think back to the last time you watched your spouse or loved one answer the phone only to hear an unfamiliar voice.

Within seconds, your loved one has come to a decision regarding this new person, and it is reflected on his or her face. His or her whole body reacts to the category into which he or she has put this new person.

This is a very normal process. It's OK. This process is generally done very quickly and at the subconscious level. We don't even realize it is happening. We need to realize that there is nothing "right" or "wrong" about this process. It's very human and quite normal. It's the only way our brains have of keeping all the incoming data under control. However, most of us are only vaguely aware of how we react to the judgments we impose when we meet people for the first time.

We need to be aware of the process we all go through as those first impressions are established in our minds. After we have known someone for a while, we sometimes change the rules and modify our initial impression. For the majority of us, if we do not trust someone or feel comfortable around them when we first meet them, often nothing they can say or do will alter that first impression. First impressions have a major impact on our lives.

How many of us can remember introducing a new acquaintance to one of our older friends? The meeting went poorly and our older friend did not like our new acquaintance, and told us so. Years later, when the new acquaintance is in jail, our older friend reminds us, "I told you so."

How many of you can recall similar experiences? We hold onto our first impressions. All of us have listened as someone spoke and have made judgments about the kind of person the speaker was on the basis of how he or she sounded. In many such stereotyping incidents, our judgments were based on the voice qualities these individuals had. In our minds, a breathy voice quality, though likable, was probably representative of a weak person, or a nasal voice quality proved to be irritating.

For years, I have observed and studied this stereotyping and the resulting judgment process. The results of this judgment process have brought many people who wanted to change the way they sound to others to seek help from me. They wanted to eliminate distracting voice qualities that caused negative stereotype perceptions. What has always fascinated me has been the impact the voice qualities have had on the reaction of individual listeners.

For over 20 years, I have been collecting data about these perceptions and stereotypes. The impact of the perception of individual listeners reacting to specific vocal variables has maintained very consistent patterns. To keep track of the trends, I often do opinion polls with members of my audiences to see how changing vocal variables will impact audience reactions on concepts such as likability, trust, and credibility. Sometime during the winter of 1995 and 1996, the impact of voice stereotypes shifted and moved more to the extremes for most audiences.

As an example, I will use the breathy voice quality in regard to the variable of trust. Prior to 1996, most audience members indicated a slightly negative or low mark by marking a "three," with some variation of course, on a scale of one to seven. During the holiday season (between November and February), the opinion data strengthened (became more negative). The responses moved to between one and two on average.

When audience members perceive a habitually breathy speaker, they now stereotype him or her as being weaker and as deserving less trust and having less credibility. Even though we may like habitually breathy speakers, we don't believe them, trust them, or find them credible. The exit polls following the national presidential election in 1996 between Robert Dole and Bill Clinton verify that information. Most voters did not vote for Dole because they didn't like him. His

**Figure 4.1**

# Likability Survey

Indicate your initial reaction to the person using the variables listed below.

| VOICE QUALITIES | Likability | | Trust | | Credibility | |
|---|---|---|---|---|---|---|
| | low | high | low | high | low | high |
| Breathy | 0 | — — — — — 7 | 0 | — — — — — 7 | 0 | — — — — — 7 |
| Tense | 0 | — — — — — 7 | 0 | — — — — — 7 | 0 | — — — — — 7 |
| Flat | 0 | — — — — — 7 | 0 | — — — — — 7 | 0 | — — — — — 7 |
| Thin | 0 | — — — — — 7 | 0 | — — — — — 7 | 0 | — — — — — 7 |
| Nasal | 0 | — — — — — 7 | 0 | — — — — — 7 | 0 | — — — — — 7 |
| Denasal | 0 | — — — — — 7 | 0 | — — — — — 7 | 0 | — — — — — 7 |
| Frontal | 0 | — — — — — 7 | 0 | — — — — — 7 | 0 | — — — — — 7 |
| Throaty | 0 | — — — — — 7 | 0 | — — — — — 7 | 0 | — — — — — 7 |
| Muffled | 0 | — — — — — 7 | 0 | — — — — — 7 | 0 | — — — — — 7 |
| Orotund | 0 | — — — — — 7 | 0 | — — — — — 7 | 0 | — — — — — 7 |
| No VQs obvious | 0 | — — — — — 7 | 0 | — — — — — 7 | 0 | — — — — — 7 |

| PITCH | Likability | | Trust | | Credibility | |
|---|---|---|---|---|---|---|
| | low | high | low | high | low | high |
| Up on ends of words | 0 | — — — — — 7 | 0 | — — — — — 7 | 0 | — — — — — 7 |
| Narrow range | 0 | — — — — — 7 | 0 | — — — — — 7 | 0— — — — — |
| Roller coaster pitch | 0 | — — — — — 7 | 0 | — — — — — 7 | 0 | — — — — — 7 |

| VOLUME | Likability | | Trust | | Credibility | |
|---|---|---|---|---|---|---|
| | low | high | low | high | low | high |
| Loud | 0 | — — — — — 7 | 0 | — — — — — 7 | 0 | — — — — — 7 |
| Soft | 0 | — — — — — 7 | 0 | — — — — — 7 | 0 | — — — — — 7 |

| RATE | Likability | | Trust | | Credibility | |
|---|---|---|---|---|---|---|
| | Low | high | low | high | low | high |
| Many pauses | 0 | — — — — — 7 | 0 | — — — — — 7 | 0 | — — — — — 7 |
| Few pauses | 0 | — — — — — 7 | 0 | — — — — — 7 | 0 | — — — — — 7 |
| Long pauses | 0 | — — — — — 7 | 0 | — — — — — 7 | 0 | — — — — — 7 |
| Elongation of words | 0 | — — — — — 7 | 0 | — — — — — 7 | 0 | — — — — — 7 |

flat voice quality was perceived as dull and boring. No one likes these qualities, particularly in leaders. The polls revealed that many voters chose Clinton while admitting that they did not believe him, trust him, or find him credible. Why is this? Voters liked Clinton. President Clinton used a very breathy voice when speaking. The breathy voice quality may endear us to people because it can be soft-sounding, inviting, and sometimes even sincere. The voters did like Bill Clinton and that's why they voted for him. However, when it comes to trusting and believing in breathy speakers, we may not feel confident in giving them important tasks requiring a high level of responsibility. Remember, voters believed they had no choice. There was only one candidate that they liked. They voted for him whether they trusted him or not.

You may want to conduct some of your own opinion polls. Copy the form in Figure 4.1 and, after mastering the material in this book, collect some data from some of the people you socialize with. To standardize the testing procedure on the opinion poll, the voice quality samples are on videotape. Contact me for more information:

> Ralph E. Hillman, Ph.D.
> 614 Woodmont Drive
> Murfreesboro, TN 37129
> 615-849-1335
> Ralph_Hillman @juno.com

# 5 YOUR UNIQUE SOUND

## BREATHY OR TENSE: SEXY OR SENSITIVE?

The breathy and tense voice qualities are paired together because they both deal with the amount of muscle tension in the vocal folds and the amount of air passing through the vocal folds during speech production. These voice qualities and the means of producing them are very important to understand, particularly breathiness. The breathy voice quality often "covers," or masks, other voice qualities so that we aren't even aware that they are there. Breathiness is also the culprit in vocal abuse and overused glottal attack. Becoming familiar with how the tense voice quality is produced helps to reduce breathiness—a voice quality that often plagues many people. Let's take a closer look at breathy and tense.

After spending the weekend doing some home repairs, you are on the phone with the local plumbing supply store to find the center post for a single-handle kitchen faucet. The store you originally bought the faucet from doesn't handle the replacements (the faucet washers were supposed to last forever). So when you call this store, a woman answers the phone in a very breathy voice. You really want to find this replacement part, so you ask to be connected to someone who knows something about plumbing. She responds by saying that she is the owner of the store and would be glad to help. What has happened here? Within seconds of hearing her speak, you perceived and reacted to the sound of her voice on the other end of the line and this greatly influenced how you stereotyped this person in your first impression of her. Her very breathy voice led you to believe that her knowledge of plumbing would be limited.

If my habitual voice were breathy, with lots of air being expelled each time I spoke, how might you stereotype me? You might think I was likeable, soft, weak, passive, wishy-washy, compassionate, sexy, difficult to understand . . . the list goes on. An audience's decision to apply those descriptive terms to me is made based on how I sound, without knowing for sure the kind of person I really am. But when we hear a breathy speaker for the first time, we think of all the characteristics of breathy speakers we have heard before and apply those characteristics to this new speaker. We do this stereotyping without knowing the "real" data. What a tragedy! But it's very real and we all do it. We make judgments about the personality characteristics of those we meet on the basis of how they sound.

## What Is Breathiness?

The habitually breathy voice quality is the result of the vocal folds opening too widely and often not making complete closure with each cycle, thus allowing excessive air to pass between the folds. In a habitually breathy person, air may be released before a word is said, during its pronunciation, and/or even after the word is said. The addition of that excess air is distracting and often makes words unintelligible. The extra air diffuses sound. Even though the sound is loud enough to be heard, it isn't clear; it is, in effect, masked. People who are habitually breathy are often very difficult to understand.

Now is a good time to make a distinction between audibility and intelligibility. Audibility indicates that the sound is able to be heard. Intelligibility indicates that the sound is able to be understood. Both the breathy and tense voice qualities are audible—-one can hear them being produced. But the breathy voice quality can be difficult to understand; in other words, it is less intelligible.

Now let's push the stereotypes just a bit. Assume that someone is speaking to you in a very breathy voice. You can hear the sound (it's audible), but you can't understand most of the words being said (it's not intelligible). If the breathy sound continues and we still can't understand what that person is saying, how do we perceive the level of his or her intelligence? In our view, their IQ may be low. This is not an indication that you don't like the person; you just don't see him or her as being very bright at the moment.

You sound different to yourself than you do to others. We hear ourselves primarily as the sound is transmitted from our vocal folds through bone, cartilage, and tissue to our ears. This whole transmission is done inside our heads. Others hear us when the sound travels through the air to their ears. As a result, even professionals often do not know that they are being breathy because they have not learned to hear it. To learn how to hear breathiness, we must first learn what causes it.

## What Causes Breathiness?

Basically, there are three conditions that prevent the vocal folds from making complete closure and are responsible for the breathy symptoms.

1. *The lack of appropriate muscle tension in the vocal folds.* These are learned habit patterns that are deeply ingrained in the muscle reflexes themselves. Since speech production is a learned skill, the habit of keeping the muscles of

the vocal folds too loose during speech production can be changed. You can voluntarily control this pattern by using a more tense voice quality and by cutting down on the amount of air exhaled during speech.

2. *The lack of sufficient muscle tension around the back of the posterior end of the vocal folds.* This lack of muscle tension results in a vocal chink at the posterior end of the vocal folds. This chink, or space, allows air to pass between the folds before, during, and after speech production. These muscles can be strengthened with the trill/swallow exercise found later in this chapter.

3. *The presence of a polyp, nodule, carcinoma, or some other pathology.* These conditions prevent the vocal folds from adducting, or coming together. They are often the result of improper functioning of the vocal folds. We will not discuss vocal pathologies in this book. Consult an ear, nose, and throat specialist—sometimes referred to as an ENT or more precisely identified as an otolaryngologist—if you suspect you have a problem you are not able to change or correct using the suggestions found in this chapter.

## What Is the Tense Voice Quality?

In contrast to the breathy voice quality, the tense voice quality is produced when the vocal folds are operating much more efficiently, that is, when the folds are not opening and closing over such a large distance. As a result, the sound produced is much louder and cleaner because much less air is passing through the vocal folds. The word *tense* refers to the sound of the voice quality, not to the condition of the muscles of the larynx or the neck. Tightening the muscles of the neck is not recommended for producing this voice quality.

To discern the differences between the tense voice quality and the breathy voice quality, try this exercise. Place the palm side of your flattened hand in front of your face touching your nose and lips. In a very breathy voice, expelling lots of air, count to five. Most likely, you can feel the excess air hitting your hand. Now contrast this with a tense voice quality. While sitting up straight and keeping your hand in front of your face, count to five again. Use a rather staccato voice, trying to cut back as much as possible on the amount of air being exhaled before or after the words are sounded. You can not only hear the difference between the breathy and tense voice qualities, but also you can feel the difference. There will be more air hitting your hand when you are breathy and less when your voice is tense.

## What about Perceptions and Stereotypes?

Now back to perception: Folks who habitually speak with the breathy voice quality are stereotyped as less intelligent than people who do not. Marilyn Monroe used the breathy voice a lot. She was popular as an entertainment personality. The impression that the public had about her was that she was not very intelligent. Her breathy voice contributed to her image as a sex symbol and caused the public to overlook any other attributes she may or may not have possessed.

You can try the experiment yourself. Try using the breathy voice at an auto repair shop, in the checkout line in a grocery store, at a noisy restaurant, or even with someone you are arguing with. Notice the response. What are the chances that a busy server in a noisy restaurant will come to your table if you are trying to get his or her attention using the breathy voice? Now try the tense voice quality in similar situations and notice the response. How does the mechanic react when, using the breathy voice quality, you begin to tell him what you think is wrong with the car . . . especially if you are female? (I am aware, however, that the mechanic could be female and that there will be exceptions to the stereotype). Most people in all geographic regions of the country will react in a similar way. Are you beginning to see what we're talking about?

Let's explore the differences between the reactions to these two voice qualities with another example. Let's suppose a younger male teenager wants $40 for a lamp! He goes to Dad first. This dad habitually uses the tense voice quality, and even though the teenager gives the best reasons and arguments he can muster, Dad responds with a loud and clear "no, I can't do that." Moments later, the teenager is approaching his mother, whose habitual voice quality is breathy. Again the teenager gives his best reasons and arguments, and Mom responds with the same answer, "No, I can't do that," but uses her breathy voice. An hour or so passes and our teenager still needs the $40. Who does he approach for a second go-around? Dad or Mom? Given the cultural stereotypes, the teenager approaches Mom because she may have said, "No," but the sound of her voice said, "Maybe."

In our culture, women (and quite a few men, also) who habitually use the breathy voice quality in business and professional settings may encounter discrimination as a result. As a consultant working with companies to improve communication, increase sales, and improve customer service, I have become quite aware of such discrimination. Very often, when females are in executive meetings in the board room and present themselves with very breathy voices, they may not be taken seriously or their ideas may not receive the attention and merit they deserve.

Teaching has also exposed me to examples of similar discrimination. I teach voice and diction classes at Middle Tennessee State University. Many of my students are young women returning to college because their husbands have run off, have been run off, or have passed away, and these women now have to support their families. Finishing a college education will allow them to obtain a higher-paying or more fulfilling job. These women have also been conditioned by being good moms to use the breathy voice quality habitually. Many of these competent, capable young women also tell me that they have a great idea for a business if only they could obtain a loan to get it started. They even tell me of their experiences with loan institutions when their applications are rejected. These women are eager to get on with their lives successfully. But most don't recognize that their voices could be the problem. Once this reality is pointed out, most are eager to learn how to change their voice qualities. I ask them to wear the same outfit they wore the last time they were turned down, even the same hairstyle. But I really coach them while they go over the very same proposal, but this time using their newly discovered tense voice quality. The results are fantastic! I almost always get a phone call with the voice on the other end shouting, "I got it! I got it!" The paperwork for processing their loan proposals has been initiated.

In an attempt to further check out the impact of the voice quality shift, I invited several male Vietnam veterans if they, too, would be part of the research. All of them visited loan institutions using the breathy voice quality as they made their presentations. At the next loan institution they visited, they used their habitually tense voice quality while making the same presentation. Loan application proceedings were initiated for all the men when they used their tense voices. None of them were given the go-ahead when they made their presentations using the breathy voice quality.

Granted, small sample. Granted, no control group. But I firmly believe that additional research would be a waste of time and energy.

What caused such differences in outcomes? Those loan officers (men and women) stereotyped the breathy loan applicants as weak and thus unable to accomplish the goals established for their proposals and unable to repay a loan. Circumstances such as these occur quite frequently, so awareness of such vocal behaviors can make a difference in our personal and professional lives.

Claims of discrimination on the basis of sex reflect a sad reality in some instances. I am not trying to defend that kind of discrimination. However, the perceptual difference between the sound of the breathy voice quality user and the sound of the tense voice quality user may be the real reason for their audiences' responses and/or apparent discrimination.

Generally, speakers who habitually use breathy or tense voice qualities are equally intellectually capable, and both groups exhibit good pitch variety. But the stereotypes still persist, and the breathy speakers aren't viewed as being as capable. The healthy breathy voice quality is so dominant that it tends to mask other voice qualities being used at the same time and is usually the only voice quality heard or recognized.

## What Is Good Voice Quality?

In this discussion of the breathy and tense voice qualities, we have tried to show the exaggerated situation for each using either voice quality. But breathy and tense are on the same continuum, just like the other four pairs of voice qualities. When working with the pairs of voice qualities, our first goal is to get you, the reader, to be able to distinguish between them by exaggerating the differences. I am quite confident that you can acquire and experience that difference by using the negative practice routine.

Our second goal is to get you to move from the exaggerated, extreme ends of the continuum toward its middle. It involves actually practicing the voice qualities aloud. For example, start counting to 10 by being very breathy. Now, as you continue counting gradually, reduce the breathy voice quality and add some tense voice quality. Continue practicing so you can hear and feel yourself going from being very breathy as you begin the count to using a very tense voice quality as you get closer to 10. Now reverse the practice pattern. Start the count with a very tense voice quality and end the count with a very breathy voice quality. This exercise may sound silly, but it's great for training your ear to hear the subtle differences as you move from one end of the continuum to the other.

If you have kept the count fairly even as you changed your voice quality from breathy to tense, listen to the sound you are producing as you count through 5 and 6. That sound should be in the middle of the continuum between the extremes of breathy and tense. By definition, that area is defined as good voice quality, where neither of the extremes, breathy or tense, is obvious or apparent.

Our third goal is to get you to use the good voice quality every time you speak. Since there are five continua, you will need to "find the middle" on each pair. The ultimate goal is to be able to produce good voice quality habitually and to use specific voice qualities or combinations of them for emphasis only when you choose to do so.

Breathy and tense are on opposite ends of the same continuum, just like the other four pairs of voice qualities. However, breathy and tense is the only pair that can be produced together. But what happens when they are produced together can be harmful. Let's take a look at vocal abuse.

## What Is Vocal Abuse?

Most Americans are often breathy when we speak. We were trained early to be breathy with the admonitions "you are too loud," "children should be seen not heard," and "be quiet!" So we've learned to add lots of air to our speech to sound softer and quieter. In other words, too much air, not enough pressure. Let's take this habitual breathy voice to a ball game so we can shout for our favorite team. In order to get our volume louder so we can be heard, we add air pressure, which forces the vocal folds to open and close harder than during relaxed speech. In this case, too much air, too much pressure. The leading edges of the vocal folds are slamming into one another hard. This condition is caused by too much air under too much pressure. Within minutes or even seconds, we begin to feel the discomfort and then the vocal folds are refusing to come together and make vibrations at all. The vocal folds are protecting themselves by not making complete closure. Our vocal folds are "smarter" than we are! If we do force our vocal folds to produce sound, we complain of being hoarse. Our only recourse is to whisper, though you'll heal faster if you don't whisper or talk at all. In the next day or so, the wounds on our vocal folds will have healed and we are free to speak "normally" once again. If we were to exhibit more control and to reduce the air flow, we could use the tense voice quality at the ball game. We could make the choice not to use the breathy voice quality at all and the damage to the vocal folds would be reduced, probably eliminated. In addition, we would be much easier to hear on the field of play, if that is our desire. We certainly will sound louder.

Another damaging effect of too much air under too much pressure occurs when we start words that begin with a vowel sound or combinations of vowel sounds. The glottal attack occurs when too much air under too much pressure is exploded out in the production of a vowel at the beginning of a word, such as you would use for the production of a consonant plosive, like you are supposed to use when you produce the /b/, /d/, or /g/ sounds. You can experience the glottal attack by pretending that you are going to lift a piano and hold your breath in preparation. As you are about to lift, force out the vowel sound, as in the word *up* or *at*. This activity forces the vocal folds to open with the explosion and then to slam back together, hard. If you speak using this glottal attack habitually, the leading edge of the vocal folds are going to sustain damage. You can avoid the vocal folds slamming together by putting an /h/ sound just in front of the vowel you are going to say. Try the piano lift exercise one more time using the /h/ sound in front of the vowel. Notice how much easier it is on your vocal folds and how much smoother it sounds. Now that you have the feeling of it, maintain the same easy production without adding the /h/ sound in front of the vowel. This is not to say that you should never use the glottal attack to give emphasis to words. Just don't make a habit of it.

The breathy voice quality is basically too much air under not enough pressure. We often add breathiness to other voice qualities to add emphasis to what we are planning to say. For example, if we want to sound completely helpless when we do the sound combination stereotyped as a whine (nasal and high-pitched), we can add the breathy voice quality to it. Sometimes, the emphasis we create can be more distracting than beneficial. Vocal fry is a good example. The flat voice quality is in your lowest pitch range and is generally very narrow in range. Count to five at your lowest pitch. Now add lots of breathiness to that low pitch as you use too much air and not enough pressure. The resultant sound should have a popping quality to it, a lot like bacon frying. That is why it is called vocal fry. We will discuss this further in the section about flat and thin voices beginning on page 44.

When attempting to discuss potentially abusive vocal behaviors with speakers, I am sometimes answered with, "My voice is fine, thank you!" Unfortunately, the speakers who say this often experience a variety of voice ailments: sore throats, "tired voices," hoarseness, loss of voice, excessive throat clearing, even cancelled speaking dates. Speakers attribute these ailments to "fatigue" or "overuse" of their voices. In reality, our voices are not tired or overused, they are abused. Speakers incur vocal ailments when they add excessive vocal tension to an already breathy vocal sound.

In this exploration of breathy and tense, it is good to keep in mind that there is nothing inherently wrong with being breathy or tense. In our discussion, I have painted a picture of the breathy voice quality as weak and the tense voice quality as strong and authoritarian. But it is also true that the breathy voice quality demonstrates likability, empathy, concern, and softness. It lets us share our compassion. What better way to say "I care" or "I love you" than with a breathy voice quality used for emphasis. What better way to get attention and/or get those you are addressing to focus on the task than with the tense voice quality used for emphasis. However, using breathy and tense together, particularly under increased air pressure conditions, will likely cause damage to the vocal folds. In fact, these factors are what contribute to vocal abuse.

The contrast between breathy and tense is often least apparent in how we express inner feelings of security, self-confidence and self-control. Then the breathy voice quality is only a symptom of a much bigger and different set of circumstances. Our posture is critical. As we'll discuss later, in the section on "The Big Three," posture has a direct impact on our emotional states. There are exceptions, but as a general rule, when we exhibit poor posture we also often exhibit a much more breathy sound in our voices. Whether conscious of what we are doing or not, we are telling ourselves and the world that we are weak and not strong enough to handle whatever is out there.

Now that we have discussed how the impact of being breathy affects our perception of ourselves and how others perceive us, let's take a look at the steps we can take toward making changes.

## What Can I Do to Hear Breathiness?

One of the first things we can do to hear breathiness is to listen to other people in whom breathiness is obvious. It is usually easier to hear breathiness (or any of the other voice qualities) in other people first. You also might want to note the values you attach to the personalities of those who habitually use the breathy voice quality.

When talking about exercises to help hear and learn to control our breathy voice quality usage, we need to remember one thing. Just do it! Don't intellectualize about the exercises; don't think about doing them. JUST DO THEM! You can't hear the behavior unless the sounds are coming out of your mouth and headed for your ear. Even listening to someone else go through them will not have the necessary impact on you.

Using the count-to-five exercise we discussed earlier is usually the best way to hear breathiness in yourself. When you count to five in a breathy voice, the vocal folds are trying to operate efficiently by making complete closure during each cycle, but they are unable to do so because of the lack of appropriate vocal fold tension which would restrict the air flow. When using the tense voice, you should feel less air passing out of your mouth and hitting your hand as you count. This exercise of using both voice qualities and of being able to exaggerate them (as well as of being able to turn them on and off) allows you to train yourself to hear the differences between the two voice qualities and to use varying degrees of breathiness (or tenseness) anywhere along the continuum.

The standing push-up will also allow you to hear breathiness in yourself. Place your feet 18 to 24 inches from a wall and place your hands on the wall at shoulder level. As you say, "Ah," keep your body straight and lean toward the wall, bending only at your ankles. When your head is a few inches from the wall, stop the forward movement and stop the sound. You should hear and feel the vocal folds close. As you approach the wall, you should hear the breathiness diminish. Now try to mimic that vocal fold closure without doing the push-up. Being aware of the sound of breathiness will help you to diminish its use.

## What Exercises Will Help Me Change My Breathy Habit?

The first four exercises below should enable a healthy speaker to learn the kinesthetic sensation of good posture and can result in good voice quality being produced. (A more inclusive exercise program is in Appendix A.) For these four exercises, you should: unlock your knees, level your pelvis, tuck in your tummy, elevate your rib cage, pull your shoulders back and down, and keep your head up. Using this good posture should help you relax the neck and shoulder muscles and allow you to be less breathy.

1.  a.  Rise *very slowly* on the balls of your feet, then drop your heels quickly.
    b.  Repeat this process, concentrating on the lifting feeling in your calf and thigh muscles.
    c.  Now, as you come up slowly, begin a count to ten. Say the word *one* loudly, with the flat of your hand against your nose and lips. If you feel any air being expelled, try again until you feel no air. You are saying each number as you roll onto the balls of your feet and are feeling the lift in your calf and thigh muscles. When you say, "Two" and "Ten," be careful not to over-expel air on the initial /t/ sound. Get to the vowel as quickly as you can. Practice and continue counting to ten using good voice quality (feeling and hearing the reduction in air as you practice).
2.  a.  Replace coming onto the balls of your feet with bending your knees slightly while slowly lifting a small folding chair or a ten-pound bag of flour.

b. Lift with your legs, not your arms and your back. Count to ten slowly as you lift.

c. Listen for and capture the feel and the sound of the good voice quality.

3. a. Count to ten slowly, maintaining good posture, while someone pushes down on your shoulders.

b. Once again, listen for the good voice quality.

4. a. Using good posture, keeping your shoulders back and down, put your hands in back of your thighs and lift yourself upward.

b. Count to ten as you do this.

(These first four exercises come from notes from a course in voice and diction taught by Dr. Paul Heinberg at the University of Iowa in the early 1960s).

5. a. Back your body up against a wall, using the good-posture steps presented at the beginning of this section.

b. Count to ten loudly and slowly.

c. Now, using the negative practice routine, step away from the wall and allow yourself to slump into the old, undesirable posture.

d. Count to ten loudly and slowly. Most people can sense the difference in the feel and sound being produced.

6. Once you are confident that you can feel and hear the difference between breathy and tense, try doing a loud count to ten as you sit down in a chair and as you stand up out of the chair. If you are leading with your tailbone as you sit down or from your chin as you stand up, you will very likely hear the breathy voice quality again. Practice until you can sit and stand gracefully without being breathy.

7. As you gain more control over the production of the breathy voice quality, try reading paragraphs and being breathy on marked words. Don't be breathy on the whole paragraph, just the marked words. This is very similar to negative practice; it will allow you to be very familiar with how breathiness is produced.

8. As confidence grows, add volume to the mix. Count to ten, getting louder as you count. Then repeat the process, getting softer in volume. Don't become breathy on the "softer" numbers.

These exercises do not remove breathiness, but they do reinforce the posture prerequisite for such removal. Once you can hear and feel the difference in production between breathy and a more tense voice quality, you will be well on the way to reducing your habitual use of the breathy voice quality.

1. Trill/Swallow exercise: To strengthen the muscles holding the arytenoids together.
    a. With good posture, relaxed neck and shoulders, and efficient breath support, initiate a cleansing breath (which is a deep breath that fills your lungs).
    b. Elevate your chin toward the ceiling. (When you first begin this exercise, you may not be able to raise your chin very high. So start parallel to the ground and work to raise it as you progress).
    c. Trill your tongue off the alveolar ridge and hum, going up in pitch. (The alveolar ridge is the part of the roof of your mouth right behind your front teeth. If you can't produce a trill then repeat the /t/ sound as quickly as you can).
    d. When you hit your highest pitch, swallow.
    e. Keeping your chin elevated, restart the trill, coming down in pitch to your lowest pitch.
    f. Do another cleansing breath and fill your lungs.
2. Echo Exercise: To reduce breathiness by producing an echo off a wall and to make vocal fold movement more efficient. This is not a volume exercise. This exercise can also be done by bouncing the sound off the windshield of a car. If you do not hear an echo, you are probably being too breathy.

    Count to 10 using a breathy voice quality. Listen for an echo. There shouldn't be one. Now, contrast that sound with a loud, tense voice quality. Listen for the echo off the walls.

    This echo exercise is also a great way to test for volume when speaking without a microphone system. If you don't hear an echo off the back wall, you are probably not loud enough.

Please keep in mind that if you choose to continue using a habitually breathy voice, it is best to avoid glottal attacks. Glottal attacks occur primarily on vowels that are the first voiced sounds of words. The vocal folds are brought together quickly and with excessive pressure to make the sound sharp and clear. You can avoid this vocal abuse by connecting these initial vowel sounds to the last sound of the previous word. So avoid over-stressing words that begin with a vowel.

3. Even though you may not think you need voice training, do a voice warm-up EVERY TIME BEFORE YOU SPEAK:
   a. Sit up straight, with your shoulders pulled back and down and your neck and shoulder muscles relaxed.
   b. Hum at optimum pitch (four to eight pitches up from your lowest pitch) at a soft volume and resist being breathy.
   c. Then, hum while expanding the range slowly up and down the scale as you get louder.
   d. Take at least five minutes to do this vocal warming exercise.

Awareness is the key. Take full advantage of this information about breathiness by doing the contrast exercises so you can learn to hear it. Listen as you practice to control it. Remember, there is nothing wrong with being breathy, just do not add the tense voice quality to it. Speakers can use breathiness to their advantage only if they know how to control it.

## FLAT OR THIN: IN CHARGE OR OUT OF CONTROL?

I'll discuss the flat and thin voice qualities together because the production of these two concern whether the vocal folds are raised or lowered. It is essential to study the flat voice quality so that we don't use it habitually on the platform. Flat means just that—a low-pitch voice containing little or no pitch variety. As authorities on our topics, we might use the flat voice quality, for short periods of time, to reinforce the image that we are knowledgeable or in control. But habitually flat speakers use only the lowest pitches available the majority of the time, and this makes them sound very dull! In contrast, thin-voice speakers habitually use lots of pitch variety, but only in the upper pitch range. Knowing the differences between flat and thin can assist you in adding interest and variety in your pitch levels.

## What Is the Flat Voice Quality?

Most of us recognize the flat voice quality by the deep, low, and often resonant sound. Initially, when audiences hear a speaker using the flat voice quality, they are interested and attentive. That low, resonant sound can get an audience to focus. American audiences stereotype a habitually flat speaker as someone who is in charge, disarming conflict, and working for the good of all involved. However, if use of the flat voice quality persists, audiences will stay attentive and interested only for a short time longer. The stereotype shifts very quickly to the belief that the speaker is dull and boring. If the flat-voice speaker also uses breathy, nasal, and/or muffled voice qualities at the same time, the audience will lose interest even more quickly.

If most of us were asked to remember professors or employers we have perceived as using this flat voice quality habitually, how would we stereotype them? Were the professors' lectures interesting? How did we feel about going back to work after discussing the day's duties with these bosses first thing in the morning? Were we motivated? Were we even paying attention? These professors may have been very knowledgeable about their subject matter and probably enjoyed what they studied, but they often failed to engage their students. These employers may have possessed good leadership skills and sound ideas but failed to create interest and energy among their employees.

The same is true for us as public speakers. We want to appear in charge on the platform, but we must also keep our audiences interested and engaged in our subject matter. We don't want audience members to remember us as boring. If they stereotype us as dull, the chance that they will remember our message favorably is very unlikely. Avoiding constant use of the flat voice quality and utilizing increased pitch variety is the best way to keep this from happening.

## What Causes the Flat Voice Quality?

The flat voice quality is produced when the level of the vocal folds is lowered. When this occurs, the size of the pharynx is changed; it is enlarged. The pharynx (pronounced "fair-inks") is the area in the throat that extends from the vocal folds behind the Adam's apple up to the nasal cavity (just in back of the soft palate). If you were to open your mouth in front of a mirror and look in the back of your mouth (over your tongue), you would be looking at the back wall of the pharynx. If you say, "Ahh," you can see it very clearly.

The pharynx is a resonating cavity, and changing its size affects how it modifies sounds. When the pharynx is enlarged by lowering the level of the vocal folds, longer sound waves are amplified and the resulting sound is perceived as a lower pitch. In contrast, when the size of the pharynx is reduced by raising the level of the vocal folds, shorter sound waves are amplified and a higher perceived pitch is produced. This higher pitch voice is known as the thin voice quality.

If this explanation isn't quite clear, it may help to experiment with an empty soft drink bottle. When you blow across the top of the empty bottle, you will hear a very low sound. When you fill that bottle half full of water and blow across the top of it, the sound will be several pitches higher. The reason the sound changed is because the size of the resonating cavity changed, just as the size of the pharynx changes when the vocal folds are positioned high or low. You haven't changed the size of the opening or mouth of the bottle, just the size of the resonating cavity. When the vocal folds are lowered, the pharynx is larger (just like the empty bottle) and a lower perceived sound is produced. When the vocal folds are raised, the pharynx is smaller (just like adding water to the bottle) and a higher sound is produced.

One last flat voice quality condition needs elaboration. As speakers, most of us combine voice qualities as part of our habitual speech pattern. When we use the flat voice quality with a lot of breathiness, this results in the vocal fry we discussed earlier. Say, "Ahh," with a flat voice quality (low pitch) and add lots of breathiness while lowering the volume. Bubbling or popping sounds will emerge.

Most healthy speakers will experience the vocal fry sensation on the last few words of most sentences. One or two "pops" is acceptable (too much air). Longer duration of the fry sound can be quite irritating to those listening and to the speaker as well. Attempting to speak louder will lead to vocal abuse (too much air with too much pressure).

The cure to "fix the fry" is to reduce breathiness and to raise the pitch level by one tone. For most people, simply reducing breathiness or talking louder will reduce the fry if the speaker is able to hear the vocal fry.

## What about the Thin Voice Quality?

Those speakers who habitually use the thin voice quality are perceived as having high-pitched voices. They may be stereotyped as immature, insecure, unsure, and overly excited. Try to recall moments when you were unsure, frightened, or really tense and the higher pitches of sound your voice produced. Imagine how others would react to you if this were your habitual speaking voice!

What are the natural reactions to a person using the thin voice quality? Imagine that I am going to read this entire paragraph to you in a habitually thin voice that sounds very much like Mickey Mouse. By the time I've read two or three sentences, how would you be feeling? Most likely, you would want to swallow, clear your throat, or slide down in your chair in sympathy for me, trying to "help" me lower that high pitch and relieve your physical discomfort. The thin voice quality can be quite irritating. When I share examples of the thin voice quality with really large audiences, they react when I bring my vocal folds down and return to my habitual good voice quality pattern. After the sound change has been made, there is an audible sigh of relief from the audience.

For the professional, continued use of the thin voice quality can be devastating. Credibility is lost when communicating important facts and concepts to coworkers or employers using the thin voice quality. Regardless of your knowledge, your achievements, or your title, it may be difficult to get people to listen to your ideas.

Currently in our culture, the thin voice quality is often used when the speaker desires to sound louder. Speakers who have good voice quality and use interesting pitch variety when they speak to two to five people often use the thin voice quality when they speak to larger groups. These speakers believe that they sound louder, but what they have done instead is to raise their perceived pitch. For example, have you ever been in a verbal altercation with a loved one? "You are wrong!" "No, you're wrong!" With each accusation, there is an increase in perceived pitch. At this point, one of you is bound to say something along the lines of "We will have to talk about this later because you are obviously out of control!" We tend to stereotype speakers who use the high-pitch pattern as being too excited or out of control. We tend to identify this behavior as shouting, even though there is no increase in volume. By the way, in the case of such an altercation, may I present you with a solution? The one who lowers his or her pitch first wins the argument!

There is at least one situation where using the pitch variety associated with the thin voice quality is a good idea. Have you ever purchased or made a small gift for someone that carried a great deal of meaning? It didn't cost much, but it meant something. You gave it to the intended receiver, and he or she responded with "Thank you," delivered in a flat voice quality. The reaction didn't meet your expectations. The recipient didn't seem as excited about the present as you did. You felt that he or she was ungrateful. The next time you get a "small" gift from someone, use your thin voice quality and at least sound excited. The gift giver will be grateful.

## What Can I Do to Diminish These Voice Qualities?

The first step in diminishing either flatness or thinness is being able to recognize what occurs physically when each voice quality is produced. We've talked about the positioning of the vocal folds and how this affects the way we sound, but we now need to feel the difference. Try this exercise to feel the difference in the raised and lowered positions of the vocal folds.

To produce the flat voice quality, simply place your fingers and thumb on either side of your Adam's apple. What you are going to do is to lower, or push down with your fingers and thumb, your vocal process (better known as your larynx). You are making the pharynx larger, thus making possible the resonation of the longer sound waves. As you gently lower your larynx slowly, count to five. You should hear a perceived lowering of pitch. Try this exercise until you are able to produce the flat voice quality without lowering your vocal process with your fingers.

To produce the thin voice quality, you can push up on your larynx. Doing this will raise the level of your vocal folds. You are making the pharynx smaller, thus making possible the resonation of the shorter sound waves. Slowly count to five as you gently raise your larynx and just as before, you should hear a change in perceived pitch. Practice this exercise until you become comfortable producing the thin voice quality on your own without pushing up on your vocal process.

Become quite familiar with the "feel" of each of these voice qualities. You should be aware of what is going on physically within you as you produce them. Do you remember using negative practice in our discussion of breathy and tense? Negative practice should be used with flat and thin also, as well as with all the other voice quality pairs. Practice flat and thin and contrast them in production until you are able to turn them on and off at will.

## Negative Practice

How does negative practice help you to change voice qualities? Negative practice allows you to recognize differences in sounds as you hear yourself making them as well as to hear the differences involved in producing voice quality pairs. If you can hear and produce these differences, you have the ability to use voice qualities to your advantage. This gives you the power to eliminate or reduce the use of certain voice qualities. When you want to say, "I love you," to your mate, you would be well advised to use your breathy voice. When you want your children to know that you are serious about the need to clean up their rooms, having practiced the tense voice quality (and possibly the flat voice quality) will come in handy. If you are a "flat" speaker, knowing the differences between how to produce flat and how to produce thin allows you to move away from total flatness and to add variety to your voice. In essence, utilizing the negative practice routine consistently will allow you to have a choice about how you will sound.

## NASAL OR DENASAL: IRRITATING OR WHAT?

Nasal and denasal just may be the most fun voice quality pair to study and work with because audience responses are so dramatic. Living close to Nashville, Tennessee, makes the working knowledge of this pair of voice qualities a necessity for me. With country music so in vogue today, one cannot miss the nasal country singer. Basically, in our discussion of the nasal and denasal voice qualities, we are talking about whether or not the nasal cavity is being overused as a resonator. Using a habitually nasal voice can be a very distracting element in delivery and also when trying to develop and maintain personal relationships.

One of my favorite stories that I share with audiences to illustrate the nasal voice quality takes me back quite a few years to a grocery store, where I was shopping for some milk. As I was bent over looking for my brand, a five-year-old came running up, bumping into me, appearing very excited. The child began looking around and pointing to the top shelf saying in a very loud, nasal voice, "Mommy, Mommy, can I have some chocolate milk?" His mother was nowhere to be found. Trust me, I know; I was looking for her quite furiously also. He couldn't see her either, so the volume got louder and his pitch kept getting higher and higher. "Mommy, Mommy, I reeaaally want some choooocalate miiiilk!" With the already very nasal voice quality and now the high pitch, he had created a very good whine pattern. What do you think should be done to this child?

Just as with the other voice qualities, many people don't realize that they are nasal when they speak. Furthermore, they certainly may not realize how irritating they may sound to other people. So how does the presence of a voice quality, particularly nasality, come about? Speech is a learned behavior. We developed our speech habits by imitating the sounds of the people around us. How we sound depends to a large extent on the people who raised us, our peers, and the area of the country in which we grew up. Most people are so used to how they sound that they don't hear themselves as being excessively nasal or breathy or whatever.

Also, as youngsters, using a certain voice quality was a way to get attention or to get our needs met (such as getting our moms to buy us chocolate milk!). If these adults allowed us to get away with our socially unacceptable behavior and rewarded us by giving us attention or what we were asking for, the behavior was reinforced. These social behaviors persisted in our communication as we got older. However, these behaviors may no longer be as effective in the workplace as they were in our youth; they are most likely distracting and annoying. The teenage girl who once used a very thin, childlike voice to get money from her father may now be an adult struggling in the corporate boardroom, trying to gain respect from her coworkers while using that same thin voice quality.

The pattern of behavior we have just discussed is known as negative conditioning. This occurs when particular communication behaviors (that are usually socially inappropriate) are reinforced by getting what we want, which is attention. Socially inappropriate communication behaviors can be defined as those interpersonal communication habits that work for us in getting attention. If these habits were audio- or videotaped and played back for the world to hear, we would most likely be embarrassed. We also get embarrassed when we see other people using similar behaviors. Like the attractive young wife in a grocery store who addresses her devoted husband in a breathy, thin, nasal voice, "Oh, snookums, can we buy another dozen doughnuts, for me?"—she really didn't intend for anyone else to hear. Her husband consented, then blushed. As he realized others had heard, he rushed on. Because these behaviors are reinforced, they become habitual and are used automatically even in situations that aren't appropriate or necessary. With this in mind, let's continue with our discussion of nasal and denasal and we'll take a look at how they are produced and what we can do to decrease their presence in our communication patterns.

## WHAT IS NASALITY AND DENASALITY?

The nasal voice quality is produced when the hump in the back of the tongue is elevated slightly and the back of the soft palate is dropped down, often making contact with the hump in the back of the tongue. When this occurs, the sound produced at the vocal folds is forced to resonate in the nasal cavities. Because the hump in the back of the tongue and the soft palate are almost touching, they have effectively blocked off the oral cavity. The sound has nowhere else to go; all the sound is resonating out through the nasal cavity. One can produce the sound in isolation simply by saying the word *sing* and holding on to the *ng* sound, the last sound of the word.

As our little boy wanting chocolate milk showed us very well, the common stereotypes associated with the nasal voice quality are whiny, complaining, and certainly irritating. How long are we likely to pay attention to someone who is nasal? How many of us really want to listen to someone who sounds like they're complaining all the time? It brings our spirits down and aggravates us. How many of you have close personal friends who are nasal? Probably not many!

Richard Simmons, the fitness expert, is a great example of a nasal speaker. How many of you own a Richard Simmons exercise tape? Out of an audience of 100 people, maybe 5 or 6 will be brave enough to admit that they own one. How many people use these tapes regularly? Of the 5 or 6 who originally raised their hands, only a couple will confess to playing it regularly. Then I have to ask those who play them regularly if they have the volume up or down when the video is playing. Almost always, the answer is "down." Then they respond with, "The exercises are good, it's just the sound of his voice." How many of us have similar reactions to habitually nasal speakers?

Do habitually nasal speakers tend to be optimists or pessimists? Other than Richard Simmons, at least on the surface, most seem to be pessimists. I would be a pessimist, too, if I had to hear myself being nasal all day. A communication behavior that sends out a message of being whiny and always complaining can reinforce a pessimistic attitude.

For contrast, and to produce the denasal sound, say, "Ah," as you would to the doctor who is looking at your throat. (Make sure you're holding your tongue down as if the doctor has placed a depressor on it). When producing the denasal sound, the soft palate and the back of the tongue aren't pulled together, so very little sound is coming out your nose. In fact, the back of your tongue is down and your soft palate is pulled back, keeping sound from resonating through your nose. Most of the sound is escaping through your mouth. Can you feel the difference from when you produced the *ng* sound? Do the negative practice routine, exaggerating the nasal and denasal voice qualities. Hold your mouth open slightly and put your tongue against your lower teeth. Now say the *ng* sound. Keeping your mouth open, same position as before with your tongue against your lower teeth, say the *ah* sound, from the doctors' office. Exaggerate as you continue the comparison and contrast. If you place your fingers on the side of your nose, you should feel the vibration difference as you produce sounds in the two conditions.

Doing the negative practice procedure with these two sounds is also doing soft palate push-ups. The soft palate moves forward/down to produce the *ng*. The soft palate moves back/up to produce the *ah*. Although the hump in the back of the tongue is moving and is necessary to produce those sounds, it's the soft palate that controls the sound waves traveling into the nasal cavity. The tongue does rise to meet the soft palate on the *ng* and drop down on the *ah*.

The denasal voice quality can also generate a strong stereotype. Most of us stereotype people who habitually use the denasal voice quality as someone who is ill with a cold. Occasionally, people who are denasal may also be characterized as slow-witted. Regardless of what stereotype may be attached to someone with the denasal voice quality, his or her credibility will certainly be low in the eyes of others. Most of us would not purchase a major appliance, real estate, a home, or a car from someone who was habitually denasal.

## What Causes Nasality?

As speakers, we certainly don't want our voices to irritate or aggravate the members of our audience. Using the nasal voice quality may do that. As mentioned before, some people don't realize that they are being nasal. Let's try an experiment to help us detect nasality in ourselves.

When we are nasal, the sound is all coming out through the nose. In this case, you can feel the sound vibrating through your nose as it passes through. Place your fingertips along the sides of your nose as you say each of the following sentences: "These books really speak to the issue." Then say, "The apples are little, but tasty." Count the number of sounds that cause vibrations in your nose and cheek bones. How many nasal sounds did you identify? One for the first sentence? Maybe two in the second sentence? Or did you hear more than that?

You should not have been able to identify any nasal sounds in those two sentences because there are none. There are only three nasal sounds in our language. The first is the /m/ sound produced by humming with your lips closed. Second, the /n/ sound is produced by placing your tongue tip on the alveolar ridge (the gum ridge in back of your upper front teeth) and humming, but this time with your lips apart. The third nasal sound is the *ng* sound. This is the sound at the end of the word *sing*.

Notice as you look again at those two sentences that there are no /m/, /n/, or *ng* sounds in either one. Since these sounds are missing from the two sentences, you should not be producing any nasal sounds. If you identified any of the other sounds as being nasal, there are several possible reasons. First, you may be keeping the soft palate down against the back of your tongue out of habit. Second, you could be keeping the articulation of most of the words you produce toward the back of your mouth rather than up front. And third, by not moving your lips, you are not allowing your tongue to move so that it can position itself to articulate sounds up front. Instead, the focus of the sound is in the back of your mouth and the closest way out for the sound is through your nasal cavity. So even though you may not be lowering your soft palate very much, there is just enough of an opening for the sound to resonate out of your nose rather than out through your mouth. Moving the lips a great deal while pulling your tongue back as you speak will result in the same nasal resonation. Moving the sound more forward in your oral cavity moves the sound farther away from the opening to your nasal cavity and thus reduces the nasality.

### What Is an Exercise I Can Do to Help?

You must do negative practice using the nasal and denasal voice qualities. To be consistent in the production of both of them, do the following:

1.  Hold your mouth open and keep it open. You may want to put your hands at the corners of your lips to make sure you keep it open. And doing this exercise in front of a

mirror will allow you to check whether or not you are moving your mouth. You can also look inside your mouth to see your tongue and soft palate moving as you make the two sounds.

2.  Gently place your tongue down against your lower teeth and keep it there while you do this exercise.

3.  Now practice the *ah* and the *ng*. Contrasting the sounds of the *ng* and the *ah* will help you feel the difference in where the soft palate is placed for these two voice qualities. You will also gain practice in training your ear to hear the difference.

Being able to detect the difference in the nasal and denasal sounds is vital in changing the way you want to sound.

## FRONTAL AND THROATY: PRECISE OR DUMB?

In our discussion of what it takes to move from a nasal to a more denasal voice quality, we mentioned moving the sound forward in the oral cavity to allow the sound to resonate in the oral cavity rather than the nasal cavity. With this idea in mind, we're going to move to our next voice quality pair, frontal and throaty. When discussing this pair, we are concerned with whether the sound is articulated in the front or in the back of the oral cavity, as well as with the position of the tongue when that articulation takes place. As mentioned before, speakers can be plagued with a variety of voice qualities all at the same time. Frontal or throaty often join forces with other voice qualities to create distracting elements in our voices. Let's take a look at frontal and throaty.

### What Is the Frontal Voice Quality?

The frontal voice quality is produced when the sound is articulated in the front of the oral cavity and the tongue is forward as sounds are produced. There is much movement of the lips in order to exaggerate the sound and keep it forward in the mouth. "Frontal" speakers appear as if they are trying to make their speech very clear and precise. We can "read" their lips even though we cannot always hear what they are saying. Really exaggerated frontal speakers often move the closed lips forward and back prior to speaking and often after they have spoken. I am not sure whether they are rehearsing what they are going to or have said. The extreme cases often hum along with the mouth movement before and after speaking.

Most of us have known a stereotypical librarian or English teacher who spoke with a frontal voice quality. These folks were probably just trying to be models of proper articulation and good learning. We often perceive folks who talk in that manner as being precise, very picky, and possibly intimidating. These are the folks who will tap the desk three times in rapid succession to get our attention or before issuing their position statement. We expect them to be right because they generally are. When we suspect that they aren't right, we quickly challenge them as being picky or phony. (We rarely do this challenge to their faces.) The Church Lady on "Saturday Night Live" is a classic example of the frontal voice quality.

## What Is Throatiness?

People who are habitually throaty also use their lips a lot, but the mouth is generally open wider and the sound is articulated toward the back of the oral cavity. As a result, the sound is often perceived as "mush" or indistinct and almost always a little nasal. The throaty speaker may sound nasal because the sound is articulated toward the back of the mouth and the sound is resonating up through the nasal cavity. Because the tongue is pulled back, the space over the top of the tongue is smaller, forcing the sound out through the nose. Jimmy Stewart is probably the most easily recognized throaty speaker.

Others that you might recognize are those folks who "chew" or "hold" tobacco products in their mouths. They keep their tongues back to hold that wad in their cheeks (so they don't swallow it!) or to prevent the juices from dripping on their shirts. Athletes also have a tendency to be throaty speakers. Athletes, when involved in contact sports, pull their tongues back to keep from biting them. The positioning of the tongue becomes habitual for these individuals and they talk "that way" even when not on the field or holding tobacco in their mouths. Because the tongue is pulled back and the articulation is not very clear, throaty speakers are stereotyped as being slow and not very bright.

On occasion, we will hear people who smile a lot using a throaty voice quality. Because their lips are pulled back to smile (generally big smiles), the tongue is also pulled back, producing a throaty voice quality. Most of the time, we are throaty because we don't keep our tongues forward next to the lower teeth as we produce vowel sounds. When we do this, not only are we throaty but also, because the sound is in the back of our mouths, we generally sound nasal.

## Are Stereotypes That Strong?

The following story will give you an idea how a strong voice quality, or any other communication behavior, can dictate others' impressions and the interactions with others. A man shared a story about his father, who apparently was habitually frontal most of the time. This man remembered his father as being a very neat person, with everything having to be in its place. If things weren't where they belonged on his desk, he couldn't answer the phone or talk to anyone until they were in their respective places. His friends used to say his father sounded like a "neatnik" when they talked to him on the phone, even before they had a chance to meet him. This man knows now that his father loved him and that he loved his father. But this man indicated that he never had a chance to get to know his father because of the stereotypes he had of his father; he never felt he was good enough. This man realizes that his father's voice communicated a great deal to him and most of it was not perceived as positive while he was growing up. This man now realizes that he is a habitually frontal speaker, and he has two kids whom he loves very much.

To avoid having a similar situation happen, this man decided to change his communication behavior. Being less frontal may at least reduce some of the potential barriers caused by communication stereotypes which are bound to be there.

## Is There Something I Can Do to Make Changes?

There is one great exercise that will allow you to get yourself to hear the difference between the throaty and frontal voice qualities. Assuming that you have an overbite (your lower teeth are in back of your upper teeth when your mouth is closed), count to five and listen to the sound. Now, in contrast, count to five again moving your lower jaw forward so that your upper and lower teeth are flush (check with your fingers to be sure that your teeth are flush). The first count to five will be perceived as throaty, the second will be perceived as frontal. In the second instance, because you have moved your lower jaw forward, the tongue has more room to move up front, and the resulting resonating sound is clearer and more distinct. Most people find that the sound difference is a real improvement.

If you suspect that you might be a throaty speaker, try putting your thumb and index finger just in back of the corners of your lips and pull forward slightly. Count to five. Now for contrast using the negative practice routine, try your habitual speech pattern (or pull the corners of your lips slightly back) as you count to five. If you are habitually throaty, you should be able to hear and feel a difference in the quality of your sound production. On the other hand, the reverse of this exercise works, too. If you suspect that you are more frontal than necessary, try pulling your lips back slightly while you do the count to five. Again, the difference should be apparent.

Another way to experience the difference between frontal and throaty is to first place the flat of your hands against the sides of your face. Now pull your tongue back in your mouth and open your jaw widely while you count to five (throaty). Keeping the jaw wide, move your tongue forward against your lower teeth and exaggerate lip movement (frontal). You should feel the place of articulation change as well as be able to hear the difference. For the throaty sound, the vibrations should be focused near the back of your mouth. With the frontal sounds, the vibrations should be occurring toward the front of your mouth.

## MUFFLED OR OROTUND: LAZY OR REALLY PUSHY?

The last pair of voice qualities we will look at is muffled and orotund. The characteristics of these voice qualities are easily recognizable and will probably be familiar to you. The primary concerns for muffled and orotund involve the use of the oral cavity for resonation, the use of facial muscles to shape sounds, and the elongation of sounds. As we discuss the production and characteristics of these voice qualities, think of examples you have encountered.

The main occurrence of the muffled voice quality is self-explanatory. When someone speaks with a muffled voice quality, the sound is perceived as just that—muffled. There is little movement in the speaker's mouth and the sound is trapped in the oral cavity. It is difficult to understand what the "muffled" speaker is saying because the sounds being produced are not articulated clearly. On the other hand, the orotund voice quality is very easy to understand. The "orotund" speaker presents a big sounding voice to his or her listeners. There is lots of movement with the speaker's mouth, much like with the frontal voice quality. The sound can be an overexaggerated, almost boastful sound.

## How Are Muffled and Orotund Produced?

When you sound muffled, you are not using your oral cavity for resonation. You are also not using your facial muscles to shape sounds, and you are not elongating sounds. In fact, since your lips and face are not moving most of the time, you don't appear to change how you sound. The sounds appear just to fall through the oral cavity. It sounds like you are speaking through a rolled up burlap bag.

At this point, it is important to make some distinctions between the muffled voice quality and the throaty voice quality we talked about in the last section. First, the place of production for these two voice qualities is different. The throaty voice quality is articulated in the back of the oral cavity, with the tongue pulled back. The muffled voice quality is generally produced toward the middle or front of the mouth, with the tongue simply not doing much movement. Also, lip movement distinguishes the muffled and throaty qualities from each other. Throaty is produced with the lips moving at least a small amount, but muffled is produced with little or no lip movement. Finally, there is a difference in how much the mouth is opened. The throaty voice quality is produced with the mouth open fairly wide, while muffled is produced with the mouth open very little.

The orotund voice quality is produced when sounds are elongated, the facial muscles are moved a great deal, and the oral cavity is used to resonate the long sound waves. You can feel the vibrations in your cheeks if you are an orotund speaker.

## What about Stereotypes?

In the American culture, the muffled voice quality is associated with laziness. In some parts of the country, when you don't move your mouth and lips when you speak, you are referred to as having "lazy lips." Potential employers may subconsciously think that the muffled voice quality is a clue to attitudes and work habits. As a result, potential employees lose their job opportunities even though they may be competent and have all the credentials needed for the job. The employer's assumption (generally subconscious) is that if applicants don't move their mouths during the interview process, they probably won't muster the energy to move anything else, especially when on the job. "Muffled" speakers may also give people the impression that they are being sneaky or have something to hide.

This voice quality can often be seen in the teenage population. In attempts to be thought of as "cool" or "laid back," teenagers will often intentionally sound muffled because they're not moving their mouths to speak. Also, since teenagers are known to be very self-conscious, they hesitate to put forth actions or behaviors that will call attention to themselves. And this includes communication behaviors. They fear "looking stupid" or "sounding funny." This can be especially true for teenage males experiencing those awkward voice changes! Unfortunately, this can work against teenagers, too, when they interview for jobs. The stereotypes of appearing lazy certainly are placed on them as well. Any belief held by an older generation that "those youngsters just don't want to work" may be reinforced by these communication behaviors.

For those speakers who use the muffled voice quality at the same time that they are throaty (and they are out there), the stereotypes can be devastating. They may be seen not only as lazy but also as stupid. Now that is tragedy.

The orotund voice quality is widely used and appears to be a favorite among television evangelists and politicians. They can be heard using this voice quality at large gatherings. They sound authoritarian, maybe a little intimidating. Those who are trying to encourage us to believe in them, their knowledge, and their ability often choose the orotund voice quality to convey that they are in charge. When you meet those same people in the grocery store, they don't sound like that. They simply use the orotund voice quality in the public forum to help them fulfill a role.

# 6 THE VARIETY IN YOUR VOICE

## RATE: HOW FAST CAN YOU SPEAK?

Fast speakers . . . slow speakers . . . number of words spoken in a minute . . . no pauses . . . lots of pauses . . . dragging on forever . . . speaking so quickly they are not able to be understood. . . . All these situations fall under our discussion of rate.

When considering how fast or slow we should speak, there are certain variables to consider. To what ideas do we want to give consideration? Will pauses emphasize my important ideas? How should this be indicated with pauses? How long should the pauses be? As we discuss these ideas, we look at rate in regard to various areas. The classic breakdown for rate involves these three areas:

1. Number of pauses
2. Length of pauses
3. Duration of syllables

One of the best ways to learn about rate is to "do" rate patterns to hear the differences. Each of these three areas provides us with some great exercises to help us experience rate differences. For number of pauses, pause / after / every / word.// The single slash (/) indicates a very brief pause, for example, at a comma. The double slash (//) indicates a longer pause, such as a pause at a period or at the end of an idea.

The triple slash (////) indicates an exaggerated, longer pause for effect. This exercise can help people who have a tendency to fade, which is the dropping of pitch and volume on the ends of words. This is often an element in several regional dialects in the United States. Saying each word separately allows one to hear the fading so that necessary corrections can be made. Fading can be corrected simply by saying the sounds on the ends of words. For example, the *ds* found in the word *finds* should sound like *dz* not *ts*. Putting / emphasis / on / each / word / like / this / is / called / strong / form. //

Strong form describes when words or syllables that are not usually stressed are given emphasis. We usually stress syllables by increasing our pitch, making them louder, and elongating sounds. To repeat, we stress syllables or words by:

1. **Pitch:** raising the pitch
2. **Volume:** making them louder
3. **Rate:** elongating the syllable or word

Remember, these exercises are for practice so you'll experience the concept of length of pauses. So to get the hang of it, /// pause for a long count /// after every phrase. /// This helps with the pausing /// and phrasing. /// Many times, /// we aren't aware of the meaning of phrases /// because we rush over them /// or we don't pause before /// or after those phrases so the meaning is lost in the larger context of the sentence. /// By adding exceptionally long pauses, we are calling attention to the preceding or following phrase.

The final exercise is for duration of syllables, using no pauses but running-all-the-words-together-drawing-out-every-sound-in-every-syllable. This should sound very much like the orotund voice quality. Remember, to get the full impact, do not pause at all during this part of the exercise. Pausing during a speech is OK. Also, concentrate on elongating the vowel sounds to help with the duration of syllables to make the sound orotund. In the southeastern region of the United States, duration of syllables is difficult for many people because Southerners tend to add sounds to those syllables, often making two syllables where there should be only one. Taking away the pauses can help you to hear the pattern you might be using and to correct or prevent a dialect from slipping into your speech. A few of us talk very fast. Doing the rate exercises very deliberately (slowing down by using pauses or elongation) can help you to hear and feel the difference in rate, which now may not have much impact on you.

As with all the other vocal variables, rate changes can only be mastered if your posture, neck and shoulder muscle tension, and breath support are all under control. Review "The Big Three" in Chapter 7 to be sure your body is ready for the rate changes you desire.

If there is one vocal exercise pattern that can help you with lots of different things, it's the rate exercise. This is particularly true if you use it in the negative practice routine, exaggerating and contrasting the old and new methods so that you can turn them off and on at will. Rate, pitch, volume, breathiness, throatiness, muffled, and even nasality can be heard and controlled by using this exercise. There are lots of reasons for the fast rate, such as: "I need attention," or, "That's how I learned to speak," or, "I don't really want anyone to pay attention to me." What matters now is that you might have a habit pattern that you desire to change.

For those speakers who use a habitually fast rate of speech, there are some conditions to consider: First, our past experiences or our mental images of these experiences with our varying needs for attention may influence our behaviors. If someone desired attention as a youngster, that person may have learned not to hesitate while talking. If you hesitate, you get interrupted and then you are not the center of attention. Thus, a person learns to speak quickly to prevent someone else from stealing the conversation. Second, tightening the muscles of your neck and shoulders by rolling forward keeps the sound toward the back of the mouth. That couch potato posture encourages fading and syllables not being stressed or even heard. Subconsciously, we recognize the sloppy sound we are producing. We speak quickly so no one else will notice. Thus, intelligibility suffers considerably; no one understands us, so we lose attention again. Furthermore, headaches and neck tension increasingly make us feel stressed, so we talk faster. We need to straighten our posture and move our upper lips. Third, we want and need to be efficient and to get lots of things done. We don't want anyone talking slowly to us because it wastes our time. We don't talk slowly because we don't want to waste time. Finally, we don't use good breath support when we speak. Quite often, we don't breathe at all while speaking. We just take in short quick gasps when it is absolutely necessary. We then use that air to push out sound (making us sound breathy) and when that exhale function is over, we gasp inhale and start all over again. Which means talking faster and "doing more stuff."

What follows is an exercise that can keep us aware of all the rate variables and can easily be remembered as part of a daily routine. Remember the following four things as prerequisites of the rate exercise:

1   Use good posture—keep the rib cage elevated.
2   Move your lips—be more frontal (or be sure to use the exaggerated frontal voice quality).
3.  Focus your breathing at the lower thoracic/abdominal area. Utilize cleansing breaths.
4.  Read loudly and exaggerate your mouth movement.

Now read the daily newspaper using the following three patterns. Read at least one paragraph following each indicated pattern:

1. Pause after each word (not syllable).
2. Pause at the ends of phrases and sentences (exhale completely, then inhale to fill your lungs before going on).
3. Elongate each word, pausing to breathe only at the ends of the phrases. Before you begin to read, take a couple of minutes to mark a paragraph from your newspaper into meaningful phrases. Then read with the elongation pattern.

## PITCH: PITCH VARIETY CREATES INTEREST

We've discussed the voice qualities and rate. Now we're really getting into the other important components of effective vocal delivery. What we need to think about at this point is how to control pitch to add meaning and excitement to what we say. We want to make sure that our pitch patterns are as consistent with our content as our voice qualities should be with our message. The most important thing for speakers to be aware of relative to pitch is that increasing our pitch variety will make us sound more interesting. Remember the discussion of flat and thin? Narrow pitch range sounds dull and boring and audiences tend not to hear the information being shared. We'll also look at frequently used yet not-too-effective pitch patterns (such as narrow pitch range, "roller coaster" pitch, and coming up in pitch at the ends of sentences) and then discuss pitch patterns that convey interest and meaning.

Elite speakers in the United States who are knowledgeable and accepted regardless of dialectal area use a lot of pitch variety and tend to follow a similar pattern in their use of pitch. They start speaking at their habitual pitch, then jump up in pitch to the "meaning chunk" (the word or phrase being stressed), and then step their way down in pitch to the end of each sentence or after several sentences (see Figure 6.1). That pitch pattern is accepted by audiences across the nation and even around the world. You can hear it on the

**Figure 6.1**

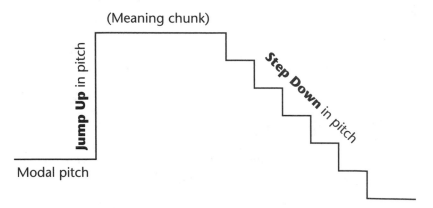

network news programs and on documentaries. Even though the same pattern exists on every sentence (or group of sentences), the pattern does not call attention to itself. People listen to it and they get the meaning intended.

Many in broadcasting are aware of this need for increased pitch variety so that they will sound more interesting. However, some broadcasters tend to overdo the pattern and use the jump-up/step-down pattern within long phrases or even within every two to five words. When we use pitch as the major method of stressing words, in a regular repeated pattern of every two to five words, without regard for the larger meaning of the sentence or paragraph, we're very likely to lose meaning altogether. That regular up-and-down pitch pattern can be very boring. Small-town TV and radio announcers are notorious for going up in pitch and then back down every three to five words whether the content merits it or not. I call this a "roller coaster" pattern. Sometimes it is up and down on every other word. This pattern, used consistently, distracts us from the meaning of the content. If we happen to be listening to the radio and the local announcer comes on the air using that roller coaster pattern, most of us will find ourselves changing stations without consciously knowing why we decided to do so.

Here's an illustration. My wife thoroughly enjoys keeping up with current weather conditions. If she is home alone and the TV is on, I can predict with amazing accuracy that the weather channel is what she is watching or listening to. She is constantly checking current weather conditions by looking out the windows or actually going outside. I think her interest is fascinating.

A few years ago, while returning from a professional engagement, we were listening to the car radio. The only station we could get was playing some jazz, music both of us enjoy. This young announcer was using the roller coaster pitch pattern. We had tried to tune to other stations, but the reception was weak or distorted. Besides, this announcer kept his introductions of the jazz selections rather brief. When he was brief, listening to him was tolerable. At the top of the hour, the announcer would be on the air with the news, sports, AND weather. What a great opportunity to check to see if my wife would be distracted by the pitch pattern that the announcer was using! Would she be able to overcome that roller coaster pitch pattern and actually comprehend the weather report? She had not heard a weather report in over an hour, and she expressed her concern. Massive clouds were forming. My beautiful bride (of over 30 years) was in weather information deprivation.

At the top of the hour, the announcer did indeed share a few commercials, four news stories, some sports scores, and finally, 35 seconds of weather. Now came time for the test. When the announcer was finished, I turned down the volume on the radio and asked my wife, "What's the weather?" She said, "I don't know, I didn't hear it." I knew she had heard it because I had listened to it. But I could not recall the information either. The announcer's use of the roller coaster pitch pattern had totally distracted us from the content. If you travel a good bit and listen to the radio often, not remembering what the announcer has said has happened to you also.

The possible changes in how people perceive us (and thus the content of our messages) caused by the effective use of pitch variety can be very pleasant. Most of us, even professionals, don't use pitch to our maximum advantage. If broadcasters and professional speakers aren't suffering from overworked roller coaster pitch pattern, they probably have the low-pitched, deep, resonant sound and don't use much pitch variety. Most of us don't find that lack-of-pitch pattern very interesting to listen to, and we are bored by the continual use of a narrow pitch range. Whether the pitch is very low, at midrange, or very high, a narrow pitch range is difficult to listen to for any length of time.

Most of us who have a propensity to have a monotone pitch pattern can rarely hear our narrow range. But we can hear the narrow range in other people. It would be a good idea to ask a friend who can hear pitch change differences to help you modify your pitch patterns. That friend can tell you if you have a problem with pitch range.

Most of us don't know what our lowest pitch and highest pitch sound like. So it may be a real stretch for each of us to find out just how those high and low pitches sound. What we are searching for are the low and high pitches that are comfortably produced without strain. Those pitches become the boundaries of our producible pitch range, available for us to use in speaking.

We need to practice using those pitch extremes so that we are able to produce them with very little effort. Since we have not practiced, producing them on demand is difficult at first. This practice is the only way those pitches will be available to us when we want to use them. Then we can begin to read (or speak) sentences using not only our habitual pitch pattern and range but also an increased range that uses the remaining higher and lower pitches available to us.

Most of us will find that adding to our pitch range will make us sound strange, at least to us, especially at first. Initially, any change from an old pattern is going to look, feel, and sound odd to us because it just isn't what we're used to. Most of the time, our listeners who know us well won't notice how we are using pitch differently. Once in a while, though, those listeners will say that they perceive us as sounding more interesting or more excited than usual.

Remember, our body as a system is trying to stay consistent and not change its routines. Our daily routine is governed by habit patterns that do not require much attention from us at the conscious level. When we attempt to alter our habitual behavior patterns, all those subconscious routines in question have to be brought up to the conscious level of awareness (inspection). Then, it takes lots of special attention to be able to recognize the differences and to reinforce the new behavior and to contain the old behavior. You must use your senses and the negative practice routine, doing the behavior the new way and the old way, until you are able to control which behavior you use (comparison). After you practice the new behavior for a period of time (correction), you will get accustomed to it and it will become part of your habit routine (precorrection). The reality is that changing communication behaviors takes practice, time, and commitment and a great deal of concentration.

Let's make the assumption that you have consciously inspected your pitch patterns and compared them to what you would like them to be. Since your pitch patterns are not like you would like them to be, we can now take a look at one way to help you change that. Let's begin with a manuscript so that we will be saying the same things in the same order each time we repeat them.

Whether you are preparing to read written material or preparing an outline as a basis for a speech, you should identify certain change options on your script. At minimum, you should consider, in addition to the pitch changes, the rate and volume changes you desire to make. You can use a variety of symbols or signs to do this. (The way you mark a script is really up to you. The markings I am going to share with you are pretty standard; they are the ones that I use as I prepare my presentations.)

Always keep in mind that pitch, rate, and volume changes are made to add emphasis to the content of your presentation. You know, for example, that you need to identify specific words, such as those in the meaning chunk of each sentence, to be marked to be read in a certain way. I generally begin by underlining the words I already know I want to stress. Words can be stressed by being made longer (rate), louder (volume), or higher (pitch). The words you are going to make louder will need to be noted with an arrow pointing up (↑) before the word. Use the arrow down (↓) after the word or phrase to indicate returning to the original volume. Then mark the words that will be higher in pitch by overlining them (a line above the word). Finally, indicate the words that should be elongated in sound with an *O*, for orotund, over the word. (And remember to use slashes to indicate when you should pause.) The words leading up to the stressed words, the meaning chunk, should be read in a relatively low pitch. Then, following this low-pitch beginning, you should jump up in pitch to the meaning chunk and step down in pitch as you read the remainder of the sentence. The last pitch of the sentence should be the same or lower in pitch than the first word of the sentence or the first word of the next sentence. Because most speakers use this pattern, it does not distract listeners when they hear it being used.

This may sound like we're just replacing a three-to-five-word stereotyped pitch pattern with a whole-sentence pattern, and we are. But the change in the meaning to be shared will be dramatic because the meaning is dependent on the pitch. Our listeners are not negatively impacted by this new pattern because it sounds natural, is used by other speakers, and conveys meaning.

Practice marking a script. Practice reading your material as you have marked it. Stretch for those high pitches and finish the sentence or the idea by ending it on the lowest pitches you have available.

As a speaker, you are now in control of when and why you change pitch rather than a slave to a stereotyped pattern of which you were not even aware. You now have the choice of what words will change in pitch, and you can break sentences up into phrases for meaning. How you want to interpret any given sentence is truly a matter of choice. How you mark your script really depends on the meaning you want to convey to a particular audience under particular conditions. How you read the script may also depend on how you, the speaker, feel at the moment. The question that you have to ask is, "Is that how I want my audience to feel about or interpret my meaning?" If how you feel and how you ended up delivering your communication is not consistent with the meaning you intended for your audience, you have a problem. My suggestion is that you plan to deliver your presentation in a manner consistent with how you developed your manuscript. Whether you are feeling ill or apprehensive should have little to do with what the audience is receiving. Stay with the plan. The way you developed the manuscript is probably what will best convey the message to the audience.

Let's look at a sentence and try some different pitch patterns. Let's use this sentence in our examples: "How high one jumps in pitch really depends on the emphasis one wants to give to the overlined word." Let's overline *high*.

<pre>
high
    one
        jumps
            in pitch
How             really
                depends
                    on the
                        emphasis
                            one
                                wants
                                    to give to the
                                    overlined
                                    word.
</pre>

Reading the sentence by following the pitch pattern indicated demonstrates the predominant jump up/step down pattern being used in the United States today. If we are used to changing pitch a lot, as in the roller coaster pitch pattern, using the pattern above will sound and feel very strange to us. But rest assured, others whom you speak to will get the meaning you are trying to share. Now would be a good time for you to make up sentences of your own and to use the pitch pattern above as a model as you speak the sentences aloud. Identify the meaning chunk. Listen to the sound of the pitch pattern.

Now let's try another pattern with the same sentence. This time, there will be two meaning chunks to jump up to.

<pre>
                              ‾‾‾‾‾
                              really
                         depends
                              on the
                                   emphasis
              ‾‾‾‾                  one
How      one                   wants to
              jumps in             give to
              pitch                    the overlined
                                   word.
</pre>

Notice that our sentence has two meaning chunks and that we have changed the level of the pitch on each. Instead of going up high in pitch on the first meaning chunk, I chose not to jump up very high but instead to wait and jump up very high on the second meaning chunk. Does that shift change the meaning of the sentence? Yes, it does. Try changing the level of the pitch on those meaning chunks. Jump up as high as you can in pitch on that first (5-word) meaning chunk, and then don't jump up very high at all on the second (13-word) meaning chunk. When you say the pattern as written, with the second meaning chunk getting the higher pitch, the word *really* should be said slowly and loudly. Putting that much emphasis on the word *really* prompts me to use hand gestures, out in front of me, open fingers, a little above waist high.

This time, overline those meaning chunks.

```
  ‾‾‾
  high
    one
      jumps        ‾‾‾‾‾‾‾‾
                   emphasis
        in                        ‾‾‾
                                  give
How       pitch      one         to
           really                 the
             depends    wants      overlined
           on the
                          to
                                       word.
```

This sentence is a good one to practice. Notice that the pitch jumps three times, but each succeeding time, it is not as high as it was previously. Note also that the last word of each meaning chunk is relatively low in pitch and that the second and third phrase end lower in pitch than the preceding phrase. Does this sentence have a meaning different from the previous sentence examples?

Put the overline on *jumps* and *overlined* for this last example.

```
            jumps
              in
                pitch
How high one        really depends
                      on
                        the emphasis
                        one wants
                          to give to       overlined
                            the              word.
```

The meaning chunks you choose are up to you.

Once you can produce the highest and lowest pitches without much effort, you are well on your way to hearing yourself and to having and using more pitch variety.

Let's continue to use a manuscript to help us visualize the pitch patterns we desire to use. To get a better handle on pitch, though, let's discuss modal pitch, optimum pitch, highest pitch, and lowest pitch. If you were asked to hum a comfortable pitch, the pitch you would hum would be your modal pitch, or habitual pitch. This is the pitch that you use most frequently and the pitch with which you begin and end most sentences. Here is an important thing to remember: If your modal pitch or habitual pitch is low, you are less likely to have much pitch variety. As a general rule, we only use twice as many pitches above our modal pitch as we have below it, down to our lowest comfortably producible pitch. If our modal pitch is our lowest pitch, we are prone to have a very narrow pitch range available for use. If we have only two or three pitches down from our modal pitch to our lowest pitch, we generally have only four to six pitches available to go up in range. The higher our modal pitch (up to our optimum pitch), the more likely we are to have and use a wider pitch range. Getting ourselves to use a higher modal pitch is no small task.

Our optimum pitch, our most desirable pitch, is generally four to nine pitches up from our lowest comfortably produced pitch (not our modal pitch). Our optimum pitch is that pitch at which the frequency of the vibration of the vocal folds is in sympathy with the resonating cavities (oral cavity, nasal cavity, and pharynx) of our bodies. Our optimum pitch feels the easiest to produce in comparison to our other pitch options, and it will be perceived as the loudest.

You can find your optimum pitch by putting your hand on your throat and humming your way up from your lowest comfortably produced pitch until the sound you hear is louder and feels easier to produce. (You may use a piano if you have one available.) If you hum up past your optimum pitch, you can feel the muscles tightening slightly, and the sound will not appear to be as loud. Somewhere between four and nine pitches up from your lowest comfortable pitch, there will be one or more notes where your "sound system" is operating most efficiently. Most people have only one optimum pitch. However, there are a few people who have a pitch range of two or three pitches, all of which meet the criteria for being at optimum pitch.

If you suspect that your modal pitch is too low and that you are not using your full pitch range, use your optimum pitch more often. Use your optimum pitch to begin and end most sentences. This will take lots of practice to get your ear used to hearing the difference and your vocal mechanism actually producing it. Use the feedback loop with the four steps (inspection, comparison, correction, and precorrection) to make the habit change.

Pitch is an amazing reality. If you begin a sentence at a pitch close to your lowest and then don't use much of your available pitch range, you will be perceived as having a flat voice quality and using a narrow range (being monotone). If you habitually begin sentences in a pitch one or two notes above your lowest, your tendency will be to use only two or three pitches above that pitch in your habitual speech pattern. If, on the other hand, you habitually begin a sentence at a pitch six notes up from your lowest pitch, you're more likely to utilize lower and higher pitches for variety. In our culture, those speakers who use more pitch variety are perceived as being more interesting, energetic, and enthusiastic, all other things being equal.

As a general rule, the more pitch variety you know you have available, the more likely you are to use it. Of course, there are always exceptions when someone begins sentences on a pitch very close to or on their optimum pitch and still have a narrow range. But if you have practiced using some of your lowest pitches and some of your highest pitches, you will be more inclined to use them. You must practice using your optimum pitch and the range associated with it. It does take practice, lots of it. But the resulting sound and the subsequent response from others should make it worthwhile.

Again, let's be certain to ensure that you, the speaker, are making decisions regarding your audience, your content, and your purpose for speaking. Your pitch pattern must match your content, your audience, and your reason for speaking.

There is one pitch habit in the United States that has been labeled "up speak." Some associate it with the speaking pattern of the California "valley girl." Some of us just call it whining. Folks who use it habitually raise their pitch on the ends of phrases and especially on the ends of sentences— even exclamatory, imperative, or declarative sentences. Many of us learned in school that, in most cases, raised pitch at the end of a sentence is an indication of a question, an interrogative sentence. But in our culture in the United States, that pattern has shifted. Now, an increasing number of questions are asked by coming down in pitch. If that "up speak" pitch pattern is used all the time, audiences are not sure of the certainty of the speaker. What I find amazing is that the speaker is not always sure of his or her certainty either. How do you respond when a sales clerk approaches you and asks by coming up in pitch, "May I help you?" Most of my audiences respond with, "No, thank you; I'm just looking."

Several years ago, I made the decision to change how I answered the phone each time it rang. I was doing it in the interest of saving time. I'm the kind of person who doesn't like spending time on the phone in a chit-chat mode. I would like to get to the reason the person is calling and solve the problem so that I can keep phone time to a minimum. In order to help in that process, I decided not to say, "Hello" (using the habitual rising pitch pattern) when I answered the phone. Instead, I answered by saying, "Ralph Hillman" (using the same old rising pitch pattern), when I answered. However, I was not aware that I was coming up in pitch as I said it. (I had been answering the phone that way my whole life, possibly to imply, "And who is this?") If I stated my name right away, people on the other end would not have to ask to speak to me; they would already know who was answering the phone. I was really feeling proud of myself because my strategy was working. I had reduced some of the initial trivial questions from callers.

Then one day a friend from Chicago called. When the phone rang, I answered it in my usually way—"Ralph Hillman," and I was still saying it while going up in pitch. My friend in Chicago asked, "Aren't you sure?" (mimicking my pitch pattern in doing so). Boy, was I embarrassed! He had nailed me good. But he brought to my attention the importance of pitch in determining meaning.

People who raise the pitch on the ends of phrases and sentences as they speak are perceived as sounding as if they are unsure of what they are saying or who they are. Most audiences find it very difficult to listen to speakers who do that. This tends to be a nationwide rather than a local response.

I spend a great deal of my time working with college undergraduates. When students come to talk to me in my office, they begin the conversation by explaining why they have made an appointment with me. The discussion goes quickly to the problem they are having with my class. In response to this, I always ask them about their academic majors and the goals they have for their lives. Their first few sentence answers also provide me with a good sound sample of their pitch patterns.

An interesting relationship between pitch pattern and "certainty" is evident most of the time. I find that when students talk with me by coming up in pitch on the ends of most sentences, I have a stereotypic response. I question their certainty about their answers to my questions. When they have no idea what is going on in my class, are still not sure about a major, and have no life goals other than to "be happy," there is a good chance that that student speaks by ending most sentences by coming up in pitch. The question, "Aren't you sure?" keeps ringing in my ears. Why is this? Because they are not sure. They tell me they are not sure. They don't like that condition, but they feel powerless to change it. Since I have talked to so many students having the same behavior, I'm feeling more and more confident in my diagnosis.

The question to be pondered as we continue this discussion is, which condition came first? Did the attitude or the communication behavior come first? My answer is that the behavior of coming up in pitch came first. After years of watching and listening, it is my firm belief that the communication behavior has more to do with shaping who we are and what we are than we ever imagined. The behaviors dictate our responses. The list of behaviors is long: all 10 voice qualities; changes in rate, pitch, and volume; and all the movement possibilities related to posture, relaxing neck and shoulder muscle tension, and appropriate breath support. Changing any one or combination of those variables will have a dramatic impact on how you and the rest of the world views your credibility. (Refer back to Figure 2.2.).

After a few minutes of talking to these undergraduates, I ask them if they will allow me to talk with them about posture, neck and shoulder muscle tension, breath support, and their use of pitch while they are speaking. I imitate back to them what I hear them saying using their habitual pitch pattern. I also ask them to imitate my body position and breathing as I repeat what they shared with me earlier, but this time by coming down in pitch on the ends of sentences and phrases. It may take us about 15 minutes to get the students in control of their body positioning and breathing and also to hear the difference between their pitch pattern and mine. With lots of encouragement, in a few more minutes, they are able to speak spontaneously using the new pitch pattern.

This realization by the students causes the "tone" of the meeting to change from one of uncertainty to one of discussing options and plans for action. We are free to discuss the matters that brought them to my office in the first place. As I listen to the students analyze their situations and consider their options and alternatives, they do so with certainty and clarity. What I contribute to the conversation at this point is to encourage them to monitor their body position, their neck and shoulder muscle tension, and their breathing as they use the new pitch patterns when responding during our discussion. They have control over the content of this conversation.

Once the discussion is winding down and they feel confident that they have gained some strategies for dealing with their original concern, I ask them to tell me about their majors, and their goals for their lives. These are the same questions I asked at the beginning of our meeting. Without hesitation, they give me those answers. When I ask them if they are sure about those answers, they reply with a strong, "Yes!" When I see them in class, I again ask about their goals. If the posture and pitch patterns remain consistent, their certainty is still strong. If the posture and new pitch pattern are gone, so are the goals.

As a professional speaker, some simple exercises may help you make similar discoveries and realizations concerning your use of pitch. First, working with someone who can recognize pitch patterns will help you. Have this person repeat back to you the pitch patterns you produce. This is often the best exercise to do so you can hear and become aware of your habitual pitch patterns.

Some people might find it advantageous to take singing lessons to help them expand their use of their pitch range. Quite often, following a musical instrument up and/or down the notes on the scale can help you hear the extent of the producible range available for speaking. Of course, any quality singing coach is going to stress using good posture, relaxing the neck and shoulder muscles, and using good breath support. All these activities will also allow your body to produce the desired additional pitch range.

Singers are not necessarily better or more skillful at using their pitch ranges than nonsingers—at least, not while speaking. If we match people according to pitch use while speaking, there appear to be four groups: good singers/good speakers, good singers/poor speakers, abusive singers/good speakers, and, finally, abusive singers/abusive speakers. For many singers, singing and speaking behaviors tend to blend together. Their posture, neck and shoulder muscle tension, and breath support are consistent whether they are speaking or singing. Then, there are the others.

There are singers who have been trained or who have learned the hard way to use their bodies and voices to their advantage while singing and performing but who apparently forget everything they know when they are talking in an interview, to loved ones, or to a large audience. Often, these singers hurt their voices more by talking than they do by singing. In these situations, the couch-potato body position often takes over and good posture, relaxing the neck and shoulder muscles, or even breathing from the diaphragm is impossible. It's no surprise their speech is unclear and their voices sound strained.

Abusive singers/good speakers always surprise me. Singers who "belt" while they are singing—singing as loudly as they can—and who attack the initial sounds of phrases they are singing are really straining their voices by slamming the leading edges of their vocal folds together. These singers sometimes appear to have vocal folds made of iron. They experience no pain or discomfort as a result of how they are using their voices. Tina Turner comes to mind.

Abusive singers/abusive speakers quite often sadden me. Knowing that training and knowledge could help them prolong their career often makes me hurt for them. But there are exceptions here, too. Louis Armstrong sang that way, spoke that way, and apparently experienced little vocal discomfort. But singers such as Chubby Checker paid the price for the abusive singer patterns. From what little information I can gather, he underwent some vocal surgery and close to replace ten years of vocal rest and rehabilitation. Now, Chubby Checker is back on the musical scene again. He has recut most of the old favorites using a good singer voice. His speaking voice is much improved.

## VOLUME: ARE YOU BEING HEARD?

When discussing the breathy and tense voice qualities, we had to be aware of volume, or loudness. As we add more air while speaking, we become more breathy and less intelligible. Push this to the extreme and we could become almost inaudible. If we are not audible, we are not heard. If we are not intelligible, we are not understood. Many times, we think that we are inaudible when we are actually unintelligible. If we think we are not being understood, most of us will react by attempting to speak more loudly. This strategy frequently fails to alleviate the problem and may even aggravate it. Then our audience may come forth with the real diagnosis of the problem: they can hear us, but they cannot understand us.

There are several reasons for insufficient intelligibility:

1. Exaggerated breathiness
2. Lack of precision in articulation of words (such as being throaty or muffled)
3. Poor choices in how we pronounce words (such as fading and stress patterns)

Before we discuss these reasons for insufficient intelligibility, we need to take a look at why we aren't hearing volume differences in our voices. First, most of us experience hearing loss of some kind. The older we get, the more hearing loss we endure. The bones of our inner ear are delicate, and we expose them, often unintentionally, to loud noises that injure them. With increased injury to the ear mechanism comes reduced ability to discriminate sound differences.

Second, we have an idealized sound which we "hear" when we speak. Many of us who hear our voices played back on audio- or videotape complain that "that doesn't sound like me." This is because the actual behavior you produce doesn't match the idealized sound your brain has been using. This is normal. We just need to become aware of the phenomenon and train our ears to be more responsive to the sounds everyone else is hearing.

Third, we are not aware of all the sound differences produced by human beings that impact our decision-making process at the subconscious level. We actually "don't know" that the breathy speaker whom we perceive to be weak may not be a weak person. Once we "know" this, we can get over the voice quality (or any of the vocal behaviors) and determine who the person really is. As a culture, we are basically ignorant of the impact verbal and nonverbal variables have on us.

Now, let's return to the causes of insufficient intelligibility. To begin, recall that the section about breathy and tense revealed that exaggerated breathiness masks other voice qualities as well as diminishes our intelligibility. Breathiness diffuses sound. That diffused sound is hard to understand. Working on a habitually more tense voice quality in your speech will return intelligibility to it.

Next, a lack of precision in how we articulate words accounts for unintelligibility. Pulling your tongue back (throatiness) or not using your tongue a lot while speaking (muffled) will lead to a lot of articulation errors. Moving lips, positioning your lower jaw more forward, and keeping your tongue positioned at the front of your oral cavity will restore clearer articulation to your speech.

A third cause can be attributed to the poor choices we make in how we pronounce words. As mentioned before, speech is a learned behavior. We learned to speak by imitating our parents, other adults, and our peers. Sometimes, they were not the best models; thus we learned to pronounce words incorrectly.

There are other factors you may want to think about. For example, many of us pronounce certain words differently from our speaking community because it sounds "cool" to us. However, the rest of the world may not be aware of these pronunciation shifts.

Sometimes we have trouble producing a clear /s/ or /th/ sound or some other sound. In order to mask or hide our mispronunciation, we simply fade off (drop in pitch, volume, and duration) on those words or syllables. We get away with fading because our language is redundant enough that people can generally understand what we are trying to say.

But volume is not just about intelligibility. Loudness matters. We can produce louder sounds in our speech by increasing the air pressure used to phonate sounds. That means using the muscles of the lower thoracic cavity and upper abdominal area more efficiently. The more air pressure used against the vocal folds, the louder the sound.

Also, if we are habitually breathy as speakers, we can achieve a perceived increase in volume by reducing breathiness while speaking. As the soft, airy sound diminishes, a stronger, clear sound emerges. It's perceived as louder.

Because our hearing loss and the convenience of closeness in interpersonal communication, we tend to get into the habit of talking softly. Then, because we don't want to be perceived as a "loud" person, we continue with the soft sound. We are very familiar with the stereotypes associated with persons perceived as loud. One good exercise is to talk loud enough so that we can hear an echo off the back wall while we are speaking. Using the negative practice routine, try talking softly, and then reduce breathiness and try talking louder with increased pressure from the diaphragm. Overexaggerate both conditions so that you can clearly hear and feel the difference volume makes in your speech production. Once you can hear the exaggerated differences, you can work to train your ear to accept more subtle changes. You can even practice this echo exercise while driving by bouncing the sound off the windshield of your car.

Some of us grew up with loud, booming voices. Everyone heard us and encouraged us to be quieter. Many of us still "suffer" from that problem; "our voices just carry." The best solution is to cut back on the amount of air pressure you use to produce that strong voice. You could add breathiness to your voice to soften the sound, but I would not recommend it. You should keep from inserting breathiness into the sound. If you are using breathiness to reduce the volume, you are not changing the air pressure at all, even though the sound is quieter. The extra air is still rushing through your vocal folds. Keep the sound you produce very crisp and clear and just cut back on the air pressure. This isn't easy. It takes practice. You will need to get lots of feedback from audience members to help you adjust to the new volume levels you are producing.

Sometimes, we think we are being loud because we are sure we hear it. Often, what we hear ourselves producing is not as loud as we believe. We are still reacting to those comments made to us when we were much younger. We need to monitor our volume constantly and to ask others to help us in the process.

# SUPPORTING YOUR VOICE

## "The Big Three"

### MASTERING "THE BIG THREE"

After mastering "The Big Three" areas of physical activity, most people can hear an improvement in the way they sound. Before going into the details about The Big Three, let's make sure we understand what they are. First, proper **posture** helps you position your body for movement and is essential for how you will sound. Second, reducing the tension in your **neck and shoulder muscles** will improve your sound as well as your appearance. Last, sufficient **breath support** will improve your sound but will also allow you to feel better. Let's continue.

### Number One: Posture and Stance: Standing and Sitting Comfortably

Our body position affects many things about us. If our posture is bad, it can directly affect our voice: restricting the breathing mechanisms from taking in adequate oxygen, restricting support needed for good consistent air pressure, changing the size and shape of the resonating cavities, and pulling the muscles of the larynx so that pitch variety is affected. But our posture also tells others and ourselves a great deal about our attitudes.

If we feel "down," our shoulders are probably rolled forward, our heads are down, and our neck and shoulder muscles are tight. We take shallow breaths and find ourselves gasping for air. We feel stress, and we probably complain of backaches and headaches quite often. If we are feeling "up" our posture is straight, our shoulders are back, our heads are held more erect, and our necks, shoulders, and upper chest muscles are more relaxed. Breathing is easier and we breathe more deeply. If we maintain that "down" posture, it sometimes makes it hard for us to maintain an upbeat, positive attitude. Who would have thought posture can do all that?

### How Can I Have Good Posture?

There are six essential components for good posture. They include:

1. **Unlocking your knees (while standing!).** Hey, we are talking about delivery and voice, so what's with the knees? Anyone with military or marching band experience can share the results of standing at attention (or at ease) with their knees locked. Those folks passed out right in the middle of formation. Why does this happen? The reality is this: locking the knees cuts off the supply of oxygen-rich blood to the brain. The muscles at the back of your knees tighten, which also tightens the muscles of your lower back. Then your neck and shoulder muscles tighten until, finally, the muscles at the base of your head tighten and restrict blood flow to your brain. Without the necessary oxygen-rich blood, the brain begins the slow process of shutting down some of its functions. Consciousness is often the first to go.

    Now, let's put a speaker in front of an audience. If a person is standing with his or her knees locked, he or she is cutting off the oxygen-rich blood to his or her brain and the capacity to think clearly is reduced. How many of us have stood in front of an audience and experienced the "no thinking" condition in which your brain mysteriously goes blank? To be the best we can be as speakers in front of audiences, we need as much "brain power" as possible.

Oxygen-rich blood will at least allow the brain power we do have to be available to us while on the platform.

2. **Leveling your pelvis and not shifting it too far forward or too far back.** This second step to good posture may be helpful to those of us who suffer from lower back pain, particularly after standing for a long period of time. Lower back pain can often be relieved by leveling the pelvis and relaxing the muscles of the lower back. Shifting the buttocks forward (or under) and easing the pressure on your lower back may pull the muscles of your upper thighs. As time passes and your back muscles strengthen, so will your thigh muscles. Sore thigh muscles are generally preferred to persistent lower back pain.

   Some folks have a tendency to place their pelvises too far forward or too far back. We've all seen people who walk with their pelvises and their buttocks rolled back and their tummies distended. Generally, these people complain of back pain, leg pain, and even sore feet. The other extreme is evident in folks who stand and walk with their hips rolled under and forward. The exaggerated stereotype of those characters are people who also wear their trousers high on the hips. And we keep looking for the plastic pocket protectors containing pens of all colors and small tools! Back pain and some bizarre social stereo-types can be avoided by leveling the pelvis.

3. **Tucking your tummy and keeping it firm from the belly button down.** You are the only one who can tighten those abdominal muscles and tuck in that tummy. Once the buttocks are rolled under (just a little bit), the tummy often reduces in size with little effort. If the rib cage is elevated a little also, pulling the tummy in gets even easier. Keeping firm tummy muscles becomes necessary to provide the basis for the muscle structure used for breath support.

4. **Raising your rib cage so that you can feel the bottoms of your ribs with your fingers (when you slouch it is difficult to find them!).** As a culture of couch potatoes, we tend to feel comfortable and to tell ourselves that we are actually relaxed with our rib cages hidden down in

our abdominal cavities. The fallacy in that logic can be exposed by doing some negative practice with a deep breath. First, straighten up, tuck your tummy, and raise your rib cage. Now, inhale and fill your lungs with air. Exhale quickly, sensing how long it takes you to blow out all the available air.

Now the second part of the comparison: Lower your rib cage and allow your shoulders to roll forward. Now, inhale and fill your lungs with air. Exhale quickly, sensing how long it takes you to blow out all the available air. Under which condition was more air available to you? If you have a normal, healthy body, the first condition allowed more air into your lungs.

5. **Keeping your shoulders back and down (this will look and feel "military" to you, but that's OK!).** For many people, the task of pulling their shoulders back and down paired with raising their rib cages makes them feel exposed, vulnerable, haughty, or boastful. Full-figured women have the propensity to carry their shoulders forward in an effort to feel more protected or more comfortable or to appear less conspicuous. Body builders do this also in order for their shoulder muscles to appear larger. Whatever the fear or need may be, it is important to remember that there are certain conditions that must be maintained to encourage good health.

Keeping your shoulders back and down will make you appear more alert. It will also allow you to inhale and exhale larger amounts of air. We'll discuss the other benefits of keeping your shoulders back and down when we discuss neck and shoulder muscles later.

6. **Head up on top (A straight line should connect your ear to the top of your shoulder to the top of your hip to the center of your foot).** For some strange reason, most of us roll our heads forward as we pull our shoulders back and down. Go ahead, pull your shoulders back and down. Did you move your head forward as you moved your shoulders? We need to resist the tendency to do this. It makes us look like we are looking for money that may have been dropped on the ground.

The biggest concern about putting "your head on top" is the difference in how you will sound. Use the negative practice routine. First, use all the steps for good posture and hold your head high. Now, count to five rather loudly. Second, let the good posture go and let your head roll forward and down. Now count to five again. To get the most from your initial attempts at this exercise, video- or audiotape the exercise or have a friend listen for the difference. For most people, the erect posture with the head held high will result in louder, cleaner-sounding speech. When you prevent your head from pulling forward, you free the muscles of the larynx to operate more efficiently. The muscles controlling the articulators (i.e., the lips and tongue) are now free to position themselves for clear production.

**Good posture needs to be checked at least once an hour, for every hour you are awake, for the rest of your life.** This sounds like quite a task, and it is. But for your voice, and certainly for your health, putting forth the effort is worthwhile. As you check your posture, remember how clear and loud your voice sounds with the good posture. This will also help you to remember to check it frequently.

Using good posture techniques is not an attempt to tighten up muscles and restrict movement. The whole idea is to use the more aligned body position to allow the muscles of your body to relax and to free you to move efficiently.

Checking your posture can be easy if you take just a few seconds to place your body parallel to a wall. If your head is well forward of the perpendicular line of the wall or your shoulders are rolled forward, you'll need to correct your body positioning. Maintaining poor posture is likely to cause the following situations:

1. The flow of oxygen-rich blood to your brain is reduced. Less oxygen in your blood means less brain power!
2. You may experience restricted breathing. Again, your supply of oxygen is being limited.
3. The awkward positioning of your body and tense muscles cause your tongue to be pulled back in your mouth. This

results in sounds being produced toward the back of the mouth, making articulation of clear speech very difficult.

4. You are more likely to speak with elevated pitch. Again, the positioning of the body is causing the vocal folds to be pulled tighter and only higher pitches are available.

5. The tension in your neck and shoulder muscles (caused by the shoulders being rolled forward) causes the arytenoids to be pulled apart, which imposes a breathy sound. That persistent attempt by the vocal folds to maintain closure while producing sound will result in vocal abuse and damage to the vocal folds.

6  Poor posture will cause the muscles of the larynx to be affected in the same way and this causes tense or relaxed vocal fold closure. Tension or lack of it limits the movement of the vocal folds in sound production.

One other aspect of good posture concerns the physical reality of providing enough room for your heart to beat efficiently. If your shoulders are rolled forward and your rib cage is pulled down, room is limited for your heart to beat inside your thoracic cavity (your rib cage). If the size of the thoracic cavity is decreased, the heart must push against the sides of the cavity each time it beats. That physical restriction puts undue pressure on the muscles of the heart and prematurely tires out those muscles. Since the movement of the heart muscles are restricted, the capacity to pump the needed blood throughout the body is also restricted. Potential problems with the heart and its arteries are very possible realities.

Now that we've got an idea of how important posture is, let's look at another exercise to help us achieve good posture. (This activity can cause some discomfort if you haven't stretched your shoulder muscles properly. I could only hold this position for a few seconds the first time I tried it. The more I practiced it, the easier it became.) First, put your hands up (palms forward) at shoulder height in the "I give up" position. Place a Hillman Handle (also known as a broom handle!) in back of your shoulder blades but in front of your wrists. This should help you to keep your shoulders in the back and down position. Elevate your rib cage and keep your head up; don't allow your head to push forward. If you cannot hold that position for any length of time without feeling some pain, don't worry. But do keep working on it. It will take a while to stretch and strengthen those muscles. This is a sign of too many years with the old, undesirable posture. Your shoulders have been pulled forward for too long. Over time, pulling your shoulders back and down will become easier, and it will relax your whole body.

The military bearing of this posture activity may feel stiff and awkward, but try not to let this bother you. You are on the right track! You are just not used to how this new posture feels. You do not need to be rigid, but you do need to sit and stand with erect posture. At first, you may think you look funny. Your friends and family may agree with you. But your audiences will prefer the more alert and attentive bearing of your body.

There are other benefits of this new posture. Those who make a consistent attempt to maintain their new posture often begin to experience a self-concept shift. Most people feel more positive about themselves and more in control of who they are, especially on the platform. When I work with clients on their posture, they remark that they intellectually understand why posture makes a difference in how they feel about themselves. However, having them produce the difference increases that awareness and allows them the opportunity to experience the difference.

In my presentation "Belief Counts: Speak with Credibility" I talk about the relationship between posture and self-concept. But to make this idea come alive, I usually try to do a demonstration for the audiences. I ask for volunteers from the audience. (It doesn't matter who it is, young or old, male or female, the results are always the same.) I will ask permission to put my arm around their shoulders and get into their personal space. Then I ask the volunteers to stand using good posture, following the six steps. Most volunteers need to pull their shoulders back just a little more and firm up their abdominal area. Then I step into their personal space and put my arm around their shoulders and hug on them. The majority stand still and enjoy the one-arm hug. As I step back, I ask them how they feel about what I have just done. Comments vary from "I like it," to "It's OK," to "Well, you were too close, but it's all right," all the way to "Yuck!"

Then I ask them to let their shoulders roll forward some and their rib cages drop down into the abdominal cavity. I ask them if I can put my arm around them a second time. Most people drop their heads and start to turn away from me. The responses to this second hug are generally quite different. Comments range from "It's OK," to "No difference," to "Get away from me," to "I'm in trouble."

Both the volunteers and the audience members comment on the observed differences. In the first instance, most indicate that the volunteers were in control of their bodies and allowed my intrusion into their personal space. In the second instance, most volunteers evidenced their lack of control over their bodies and my apparent control over them as I intruded into their personal space.

To further illustrate the point, I ask the volunteers to step across the platform so that they are about 20 feet away from me. I again ask them to face me and resume a stance using good posture. I ask them if I may look at them while they are using good posture and then again when they are using a "couch potato" stance. Receiving their consent, I think about blue skies, count to 10, and look in their direction from their feet all the way to their head. When I am finished, the volunteers respond to the differences.

Volunteers report that my looking at them while they are using good posture caused them few, if any, problems. Many see the look as a compliment on their good looks. The volunteers generally feel in control of the situation. While the volunteers are in their relaxed posture with their shoulders rolled forward, the comments are not as positive. Many volunteers report that they felt invaded. Some felt like covering themselves with their hands. Most felt vulnerable and out of control.

As the one doing the looking, I try to keep the "look" the same. I am concentrating on blue skies, counting to 10 as I gaze in their direction. Audiences report that I am consistent with both sets of looks. What made the dramatic difference in the volunteers' reactions and responses?

I believe quite strongly that it is the muscle tension in the upper shoulders that alters our self-concept and introduces too much harmful stress into our lives. Tension in your upper shoulder muscles impacts how you view yourself (self-concept) and changes or affects the meaning you attach to incoming data. How we assign meaning to what is happening around us will determine how we react to it. Our reaction is also a major ingredient in what we may experience as stress. How many of us have heard someone say, "It is not what happens to you that stresses you out, it is how you react to what is happening to you that stresses you out." When we are standing erect, we are more likely to have a strong, positive self-concept. We feel in control and capable of interacting with our peers. A "couch potato" posture will not help us feel in control and may make us feel we need either to defend ourselves or to run and hide.

This is consistent with what I learned while teaching speech classes in prisons. Inmates reported that the best victims for robbery are those who stand and walk with this slouched posture. They appear timid and vulnerable to their surroundings. The inmates further informed me that they are less likely to attack those standing up straight who have an air of confidence. These people usually result in less successful robberies because they are alert and more aware of their surroundings. It seems more difficult to catch them off guard.

In self-esteem programs being used in elementary and high schools across the nation is the call to "Stand Up, Speak Out." The cry of these programs probably reflects what we have been discussing about posture. If students are "standing up" they are going to feel more in control, more capable of speaking out and saying "no" to drugs and other social pressures around them.

### Discovering Our "Home Position"

Let's talk about the influence posture has on an audience's feelings about a speaker. Let's take two extremes to illustrate my point. Roll your shoulders forward and let your arms hang in front of your body with your head and eyes pointed toward the floor. Now you look depressed and unprepared. Your audience won't be satisfied with this appearance or particularly eager to hear your message. People will not be as willing to trust you. And you probably won't feel very happy with yourself or the way your audience will react to you.

With your shoulders rolled forward and your arms swinging in front of you, the backs of your hands will be forward as you swing your arms while you walk. (Someone ought to throw you a banana; they will have found the "missing link.") Humanoids who stand upright tend to walk with their thumbs forward as their arms swing freely from their sides when they walk. Try the contrast. How will audience response differ when we use these two different posture models? Credibility is at stake. Most of us need to work on our posture.

Let's go to the other extreme. This time, mimic the rigid, chest-puffed-up, military posture. Hold your head up and back so that you are really looking down your nose at the audience. Audience members might be pleased with the perceived confidence you are exhibiting, but it is unlikely that they will be able to identify with you or really get into your message. This posture won't make you happy either; it may make you feel uncomfortable.

The goal is to be somewhere in between these two extremes, leaning slightly toward the military stance. Once you check your posture by backing your body up against a wall, plant your feet about shoulder-width apart. Resist the temptation to shift your weight from one leg to another. Most of us will need to practice standing erect with our shoulders back and our hands down at our sides while maintaining equal weight on both feet. This stance is the most unobtrusive posture you can use on stage. Call this posture the **home position,** the one you return to between gestures and movements.

Asking a group of people to stand for five minutes using this home position will help exaggerate the difficulty of maintaining this stance. Most of the group won't be able to sustain it for more than a minute or so. We are so used to using the couch potato posture, which tells us that we are relaxed or "cool." We may not be telling our audiences that we are relaxed or cool. They may see us as sloppy, unprepared, and possibly suffering from stage fright.

## Number Two: Relaxing Neck and Shoulder Muscles

Relaxing neck and shoulder muscles, though a separate idea, goes hand in hand with good posture. It is important to avoid tension of the muscles on the front and sides of your neck. Tightness in the neck and shoulder muscles will affect the functioning of the vocal folds. Even though we may stand up straight and appear relaxed, it is still very possible to have our neck and shoulder muscles in an undesired and tensed condition. In that tensed condition, we make ourselves vulnerable to the forces around us. So remember, when checking your posture, make sure you relax your neck and shoulder muscles. Put your hand to your neck to feel the tension while breathing and speaking or watch for tension in a mirror or on video. When the neck and shoulder muscles are tight, the muscle movement in and around the larynx is inhibited.

Many of us have a habit of tightening the neck muscles when we make a mistake or feel uncomfortable. This neck pull is often accompanied by a brief noisy inhale. When we do a neck pull, we are also tightening the shoulder muscles and generally the muscles of the upper chest. Not only are neck pulls ugly, but also they easily become habits that we do even when there is no stimulus.

I often demonstrate neck pulls for my audiences. On the way home an hour or so later, I can feel my body generating a neck pull. This neck pull had no immediate stimulus. The only stimulation was the demonstration about an hour before. Neck pulls tend to feed on themselves, entering our feedforward system very easily and becoming habits very quickly. Several associates to whom I explained this revelation experienced the same results. They had never done neck pulls as part of a habit routine that they were aware of. Each of them experienced an unsolicited neck pull within an hour or so of doing a couple of neck pulls as a demonstration.

Many speakers maintain this tense neck and shoulder muscle condition because they are often not aware the condition exists. Others believe that positioning their bodies with their heads and shoulders pulled forward indicates emotional interest and concern about the audience they are addressing. People who put their heads forward as they smile or nod approval keep the muscles of their neck and shoulders tight and tend to remain in that tensed condition. The appearance of these speakers resembles that of a robin, a goose, or a turtle. Some of them nod so much that they remind us of the dog with the bouncing head often seen in the rear windows of automobiles. This body positioning may be creating delivery and health problems for these speakers.

### Facial Blush

There are speakers who experience a facial blush when they are fearful, believe they have messed up, or feel on the spot. Often this blush is a full-body flush. They can feel and their audiences can see the redness creep up their necks and take over their faces. If this condition plagues you, try moving your body into a good posture stance. As you feel the flush affecting your body, raise your rib cage and pull your shoulders back and down as you keep your head up and back.

Keeping those shoulders back and down, take a big cleansing breath. Speakers who experience the dreaded flush are elated when they find they can terminate its onset. By holding the posture and continuing the cleansing breaths, they find that they can make the red recede back down the neck.

### Number Three: Breath Support— Learn To Take A Cleansing Breath

For proper breath support, we are looking to use diaphragmatic breathing. Diaphragmatic breathing involves using the muscles of the diaphragm, which attach at the base of the rib cage and hump up into the chest cavity. When you are breathing most efficiently, the muscle activity and movement will be around the torso between the navel and the base of the sternum. The ribs should rise slightly and move sideways. Keep the tummy firm from the navel down, expanding the rib cage sideways. Use the upper abdominal muscles without raising the shoulders or puffing out the lower abdominal cavity. (Our lungs are not down there!)

There are many authors who have lots of advice on the most efficient way to breathe. I offer the following as evidence. Take notice of the articles in popular magazines that are displayed on the endcaps as you go through the grocery store checkout. In many articles about stress, authors present tips and advice on good breathing. Some advise you to raise your shoulders for better breathing. Others suggest that you distend your abdominal cavity. Then there will be the articles that tell you to take in short breaths of air to give you an extra "boost" or to take deep breaths to replenish your oxygen supply. Most of this advice needs to be put to the test. Readers should ask, "Does it really work like they say it will? Am I getting more air in my lungs? Is this method encouraging or increasing the oxygen exchange?" AND they should ask, "How do I look and feel while I am doing this particular breathing pattern?"

Allow me to share some realities regarding your breathing mechanisms as I see them. Generally, there are four physical areas that we can move to get air into our lungs: clavicular, upper thoracic, lower thoracic/abdominal, and abdominal. It's important to understand these areas in order to adjust our body activity accordingly. Refer to Figure 8.2 (p. 115) for a visual diagram.

First, moving the clavicular area involves raising and lowering your shoulders (and little else) when you inhale/exhale. For sufficient breath support for efficient speech, this type of breathing does little for you. However, if you want an exercise to increase the size of your shoulder muscles, this is perfect! As a speech professional concerned with reducing muscle tension in your neck and shoulders for better vocal communication, the idea of raising your shoulders every time you inhale certainly is bothersome. I also believe it looks funny to everyone you are talking to.

This constant movement of the shoulders tightens those muscles and results in tight neck muscles, and this, in turn, means the muscles of the vocal folds are being affected. The tight neck muscles restrict the movement of the larynx and the vocal folds themselves. This could result in a more narrow pitch range and excessive breathiness. Because the neck muscles are tight, the muscles of the lower jaw and the tongue are also tight. The muscles of the tongue are being pulled out of proper position each time speech is attempted. The resulting sound is usually that of slurred speech and the throaty and/or muffled voice qualities. Furthermore, it takes a lot of work to get the minimal amount of breath support provided by clavicular breathing.

What does all this shoulder movement do for your visual image? Your voice is critical and you need to have breath support to be able to speak in a fashion that will not distract your audience from your message. But just think for a moment about how ridiculous you look as you raise your shoulders to breathe 12 to 18 times a minute. You will look like you are gasping for air, and that is exactly what you will be doing. This is not a very pleasant image, particularly if you are speaking in front of an audience. The folks in your audience may not make the connection at the conscious level (they are trying to listen for your content), but subconsciously, they are going to be worried about your physical well-being. "Are you going to live?" becomes the significant question for them.

The second area of breathing, the upper thoracic area, is used when you raise and lower your rib cage while inhaling. To provide you with an example of this, imagine that you are using free weights to strengthen your upper arms. You've got your weights in hand, and you're set to start your repetitions. To prepare yourself, you raise your rib cage and your shoulders are back and down; you are "locked" into position. As you take a deep breath, your rib cage is raised as you fill your lungs. This is utilizing the upper thoracic area for respiration.

Before we move onto the third area of breathing, try some negative practice. Contrast clavicular breathing with upper thoracic breathing. Can you tell a difference in the quantity of air you receive?

The next area for breathing is the lower thoracic/abdominal area. When you use this area for breathing, the rib cage rises toward the front and the ribs are expanded out sideways. Most of the movement is between the base of your sternum and your navel. To understand how this breathing works, stand erect with good posture. Place your hands on your sides directly below your shoulders at the base of your ribs and push hard toward the middle against your ribs. Expand your ribs outward to the sides against the pressure of your hands to inhale air. Make the ribs spread as they rise in front slightly. Be sure to keep the abdominal muscles firm. Putting your hand at the base of your sternum should allow you to feel your ribs separate as you inhale from the lower thoracic/abdominal area. Again, use negative practice to contrast this area of breathing with the previous two breathing areas.

The last area of breathing for us to discuss is the abdominal area. Breathing from the abdominal area involves expanding and contracting the lower abdomen. Roll your shoulders forward slightly and let your ribs sink into your abdomen. Now inhale by expanding the lower abdominal area below your navel. Notice how much energy it takes to get even a small amount of air into the lungs.

Again, compare and contrast all four areas of respiration. Most people who do this exercise report that the lower abdominal/thoracic area yields the largest air exchange. I strongly recommend this area for habitual breathing. I refer to breathing from the lower thoracic/abdominal area as diaphragmatic breathing.

But I must caution you that other writers call their favorite area of breathing diaphragmatic breathing too. So be aware as you compare the two methods. They may be very different.

For those whose posture and breathing habits leave them with the propensity to breathe from the lower thoracic/abdominal area, I'll give a word of caution in this anecdote. My mother was diagnosed with tuberculosis shortly after I was born. She spent three and a half years in a sanitarium taking "the cure." This consisted of lying perfectly still in bed with sand bags on her chest for 23 hours a day. Her tuberculosis went into remission.

Because of the disease, the treatment, and fear of coming out of remission, she chose not to breathe using her rib cage. Her only choice was to breathe by dropping her intestines and expanding her abdominal cavity each time. In her later years, she suffered a condition diagnosed as twisted colon. The colon was loose in the abdominal cavity and twisted around itself. Surgery was required to untwist it and, in her case, a section had to be removed. The surgeon assured me that the procedure was perfectly safe and that she would heal completely and be able to resume life as she had known it before. All of that proved to be true.

I questioned the surgeon regarding the cause of the twisted colon. He didn't know, nor did he seem too interested. I proposed that the reason the intestines were loose and free to twist was because the vicara (connecting tissue keeping the intestines in place) had been torn because my mother was habitually pushing down on them every time she breathed. The intestines were therefore free to twist rather than be held in place.

Now, as doctors become increasingly aware of prevention, my theory is at least being heard. But to my knowledge, there have been no long-term studies using control groups to test it.

### Cleansing Breaths

To obtain the most value from diaphragmatic breathing, use a cleansing breath, which can be a valuable stress-reduction tool. Dr. Richard Quisling, Summit Medical Center, Donelson, Tennessee, calls this a cleansing breath because it provides the lungs and your body with the cleansing effect of more oxygen.

Performing a cleansing breath is simple: Keeping your posture erect (head up with shoulders back and down) and relaxing your neck and shoulder muscles, completely fill the lungs, allowing the air to enter through your nose freely and easily expanding the rib cage sideways. Now, pursing your lips, completely empty your lungs BY FORCING THE AIR OUT by blowing through pursed lips, keeping the exhaled air under pressure by using your diaphragm—lower and contract the rib cage. To know that you are getting the full benefit of a cleansing breath, place your hands around your abdominal area at the base of the ribs. You should feel this area moving in and out, expanding sideways. Now repeat and do another cleansing breath. A cleansing breath will relax your spirit, your voice, and your body.

Why blow out the air from a cleansing breath by forcing it out under pressure? Inside your lungs is a membrane that allows oxygen to be exchanged for carbon dioxide. From infancy up to the age of about 12 years, the membrane makes the oxygen exchange using the available air in the lungs. Somewhere between the ages of 12 and 22, that membrane matures and thickens, making the oxygen exchange more difficult without increasing the air pressure against the membrane. The body responds by doing a bigger than average inhale every five to eight minutes. During this bigger inhale, the air in the lungs is forced against the membrane, allowing more oxygen exchange. Most of the time, this heavy inhale and corresponding sigh/exhale is accompanied by some shifting of body position.

You can time the occurrences of these bigger inhales and exhales in yourself. It is easiest to do on yourself while listening to a speaker or watching TV. Most of us will be surprised at the regular pattern our body uses to ensure an adequate oxygen supply for our brain and the rest of our body.

The following is a breathing contrast exercise: Test the impact of the oxygen exchange when doing a cleansing breath. Do four cleansing breaths in a row with lip constriction and lots of air pressure from the diaphragm. After you have done the four cleansing breaths, note the strong possibility that you are experiencing a head rush. Now, for contrast, using The Big Three, fill your lungs and gently release the air with no constrictions and minimal air pressure. No head rush!

By forcing out the air, you are encouraging a greater oxygen exchange in your lungs and getting more oxygen in your blood. That oxygen rich blood is spread throughout your body and some of it actually makes its way to your brain. The benefits of additional oxygen in your brain should be obvious. Regular cleansing breaths strengthen the diaphragm muscles, providing more breath support for speech.

To illustrate how vital The Big Three can be, allow me to share a story about the impact that posture, neck and shoulder muscle tension, and breath support have had on the life of one person. The following story gets played over and over again with different individuals I encounter, so it may apply to you also. This person is 20 years old and she has sung and spoken in public quite a bit. She has also won several local beauty pageants. She was referred to me because she became extremely nervous and physically ill when she had to speak in public. As we began to talk about the problem, it became obvious that each time she spoke, she moved her head forward slightly. She explained that no one had ever noticed this before, but she explained that it was her way of showing the people she addressed that she cared for them and their concerns. For her, it was her way of showing empathy, just as many other speakers attempt to do.

However, each time her head came forward, the muscles in the front of her neck also tightened up slightly. The top of her shoulders also rolled forward a bit, and her rib cage lowered ever so slightly. As a result, her rib cage had limited room to expand so that her diaphragm could operate efficiently. Instead, she was raising her shoulders and expanding her lower abdominal cavity by distending her tummy each time she took a breath. As she spoke, her physical appearance became more awkward and consequently caused more discomfort. But for our young beauty queen, the most significant damage was taking place in her self-concept. She felt very insecure, vulnerable, and quite sure that I disapproved not only of what she was saying but also of how she was saying it. Although she could not cite any specific data that may have validated these feelings (such as how I looked at her or what I said to her), she still had those feelings.

I talked to her about The Big Three. I explained each of the concepts and asked her to implement each of them. Finally, she was able to feel the difference between using her old posture and the new, more appropriate posture. I had her stand with the back of her head touching the wall. When she stood up straight and freed her body to work more efficiently, she first noticed how different her voice sounded. The sound was clearer and louder; it was less breathy and more frontal. She was also using more pitch variety. When she spoke about her singing career using The Big Three, she looked at me and said, "You like how I look and sound, too, don't you?"

Since I anticipated that this revelation was coming, I had been careful not to change my facial expressions or my body position. I wanted her to realize on her own the difference in how she perceived herself. But I did agree with her. By using The Big Three, she had changed how she viewed herself and, thus, she changed how I viewed her. The change was really spectacular. She had been referred to me because she needed help getting over her fear of speaking in public. We never talked about giving speeches, but she left not fearing them.

### Stress Workshop

Like many professional speakers, I have conducted stress workshops, from a couple of hours to a full day long. There is some really interesting material out there regarding stress and how to handle it. Watching and talking to the participants at my workshops, I have come to some conclusions regarding stress. Believing you have the power to refocus your thinking and your body tension is a start toward focusing your mind on other things. *Believing* you have the power is mandatory. Finally, **breathe.** Do cleansing breaths! Utilize The Big Three. Concentrate on slowing down the inhales and exhales. Start with 5-second inhales and 5-second exhales. Practice those for a while. Then practice 10-second inhales and 10-second exhales. Watch the clock and concentrate on inhaling as much as you can and then completely blowing out as much air as you can. As you exhale, blow the air out under pressure. Encourage as much oxygen exchange in your blood stream as possible.

Voila! A stress workshop.

When experiencing stress, **breathe.**

Now, I am not saying that other methods of reducing stress aren't equally as good. Nor am I saying you shouldn't try them. This posture/breathing stress workshop is cheap, convenient, and easy. It also works for a lot of people. Give it a try! It might work for you.

# YOUR VOCAL EQUIPMENT

## Sound Comes from Where?

To gain an understanding of the source of sound known as speech, we need to look at the four basic systems involved (see Figure 8.1):

1. The **respiratory system,** which supplies the air pressure for speech
2. The **phonatory system,** which provides the sounds of speech
3. The **resonatory system,** which amplifies and augments the intensity of the tones of speech
4. The **articulatory system,** which shapes the sounds of speech

### THE RESPIRATORY SYSTEM: BREATHE DEEPLY

The brain starts the whole speaking process with a message to one of the habit routines in the feedforward system. The brain then forwards this command to the muscles of the vocal folds to contract (to pull together). Once the vocal folds come together, they are held together by muscle tension that keeps air from escaping as air pressure builds. The brain then calls for air pressure, which will increase as the diaphragm forces air up against the vocal folds to increase subglottal pressure. (The

**Figure 8.1**

# Four Systems

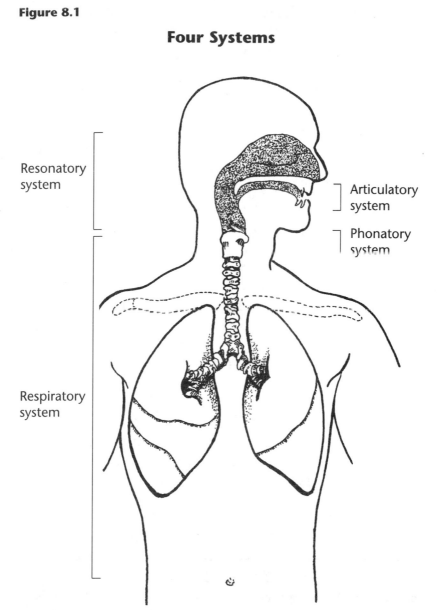

diaphragm is the primary muscle used for breathing.) This is a very simple explanation; there is actually a lot more to it.

There are four physical areas of respiration: clavicular, upper thoracic, lower thoracic/abdominal, and abdominal (see Figure 8.2). By discussing each of these areas, we will be better able to ascertain how to use the body parts involved in respiration most efficiently for better health and for speech. As we compare the four areas of breathing, we will look at the ability or inability of each to provide sufficient breath support.

We all know that our lungs lie within our ribcages. The lungs aren't muscles capable of movement. They contain muscle tissue, but they do not work like muscles. The lungs are made of a fibrous, porous, spongelike material. Having residual air—the constant supply of air within our lungs that we can't empty out by exhaling—in the lungs gives them their shape. Often we see athletes lose consciousness after being elbowed. This is the well-known act of having "the air knocked out of you."

Inhalation and exhalation are accomplished by using the diaphragm muscle and the connecting muscles of the ribcage, the intercostals. When the brain sends the command to breathe, the external intercostal muscles raise the ribs, expanding the cavity up in front and out on the sides. Meanwhile, the diaphragm contracts downward. The diaphragm is attached at the base of the ribs, humps up into the thoracic cavity or rib cage, and is the wall separating the thoracic cavity from the abdominal cavity. With the ribs moving up and out and the diaphragm moving down, a vacuum is created inside the thoracic cavity and air rushes in to equalize the pressure. The lungs are like sponges attached to the walls of the ribcage. They just accept the air.

In children, as the air enters the lungs, oxygen is freely exchanged for carbon dioxide. This exchange takes place in the alveoli, microscopic air sacs in the membrane that line

**Figure 8.2**

# Respiratory Systems

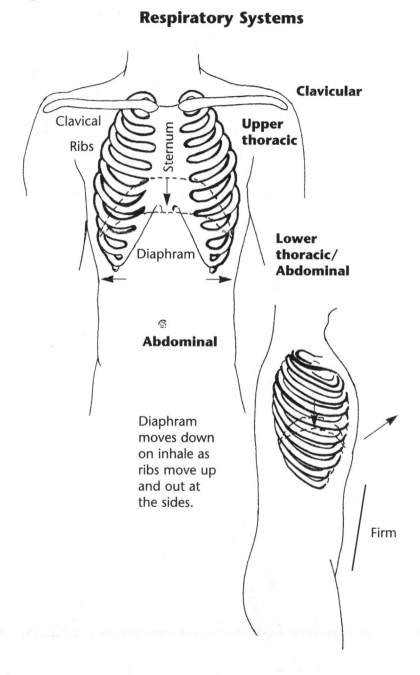

Clavicular

Clavical

Ribs

Sternum

Upper thoracic

Diaphram

Lower thoracic/ Abdominal

Abdominal

Diaphram moves down on inhale as ribs move up and out at the sides.

Firm

the inside of the lungs. At some point after the age of 12, this membrane begins to thicken and free access to the alveoli is more difficult. The critical exchange of gases in the alveoli is now accomplished during the exhale part of the cycle. The pressure of the ribcage, the diaphragm, and the intercostal muscles forces the air out of the lungs. This forcing of air is needed to put pressure on the air in the alveoli, encouraging the absorption of oxygen from the fresh air and the removal of carbon dioxide from the blood. As we get older, we abuse the membrane in our lungs with smoke and other contaminants. As it thickens, more air pressure is required to accomplish the necessary oxygen exchange.

In order to maintain an adequate oxygen supply in our bodies, cleansing breaths are required. When exhalation begins, the internal intercostal muscles and the diaphragm contract to force air into the alveoli sacs and to force the air laden with carbon dioxide out of the lungs. Refer to Chapter 7 to learn how to execute a cleansing breath to force that oxygen exchange.

We do our inhale/exhale routine 12 to 18 times a minute. Every three to eight minutes of relaxed breathing, we can feel a larger inhale. That is the result of our brain reacting to our lowering oxygen supply by increasing the length of the inhale, thus creating more pressure on the exhale. This forces the exchange, so the oxygen supply is replenished. If a person's lung membrane is really thick, the heavy inhales need to be bigger and more frequent because the oxygen exchange is getting less and less efficient. This is the reality in the medical condition called emphysema, the smoker's wheeze and cough.

Have you ever been in the same room with a sleeping adult? Let's assume that you and that adult have just had some kind of verbal altercation. You are still awake when he or she falls asleep. Within the first few minutes, you hear the person take a deep inhale, then exhale. Because it is a deep

inhale/exhale it is also noisy. You may be thinking that he or
she is responding out of an emotional reaction toward you.
You think the person is still angry or upset with you. Not
true. He or she is actually breathing to stay alive. In reality,
the person is taking a cleansing breath to renew the body's
oxygen supply.

Now, back to the areas that we habitually use to breathe.
If you are using the clavicular area, you are raising your
shoulders each time you inhale. Try it. If you are sitting like a
couch potato, with your rib cage down into your abdominal
cavity, your shoulders and lower abdominal areas are the only
things free to move. As you do noisy inhales and exhales, listen to the length of time it takes you to do one exhale. Let's
refer to that length of time as one unit.

The second area for respiration is the upper thoracic area.
Weight lifters and body builders will raise their ribcages to
give them a foundation as they approach weigh machines to
work on their forearms or to do wrist curls. There are a lot of
people who breathe using that same kind of movement. It
takes a lot more energy than is really necessary, but it doubles
the capacity of the lung cavity that the clavicular area provides. Do some serious upper thoracic breathing. Do a noisy
exhale to check the amount of time it takes to do one. Upper
thoracic area breathing will generally generate two units as
compared to the one unit for the clavicular area.

The third area is the lower thoracic/abdominal area. The
movement for this area of breathing will be above the belly
button and below the sternum. As you practice this one, keep
your posture erect with your shoulders back and down. As you
inhale, expand the ribcage forward and sideways. Place your
hands on the base of your ribs on both sides of your body.
Push hard against your ribs as you tighten your intercostals
and expand your ribs sideways while you inhale. Your
diaphragm will tighten and lower itself without any coaching.

If you are normally a clavicular or abdominal breather, you might have to exert a great deal of pressure against your ribs to even get them to move at first. If you already breathe using this area, this will be a very easy exercise. Do several repetitions before you do a noisy exhale so that you can time it. Most people find that this area of breathing will yield three and sometimes four units of air. That is twice as much as the upper thoracic area, and three or four times as much as the clavicular area. If you want to get really scientific, use the hardware that measures vital capacity and experiment with these three areas of breathing. It will make a believer out of you. It did me.

My wife and I do foster care for newborns through several church-related adoption agencies. As of this writing we have had the opportunity to participate in the lives of more than forty infants. We have had plenty of opportunities to observe the methods babies use to breathe. Human beings come "out of the tube" breathing naturally utilizing the lower thoracic/abdominal area for breathing. All things being equal, each of us had that same capacity as a breather. Somewhere along the line some of us chose to change that very natural pattern for breathing with some other area (such as the shoulders) being more prominent. Now you know the rest of the story and you have the opportunity to change should you choose to do so.

We do have one more area of breathing to discuss, the abdominal area. Each time you inhale using this area, you push out your abdominal area below the belly button. Each time you exhale, pull the abdominal muscles back in. Not only does abdominal breathing provide you with minimal air for breathing, it is not very attractive to see someone's stomach pulsating in and out! Make sure you practice these a few times before you do a noisy exhale to establish a time unit. Most people only get one unit of air.

While discussing the use of these four areas for respiration, I hope I have been successful in sharing my bias for the lower thoracic/abdominal area as the preferred area. I refer to breathing from this area as diaphragmatic breathing. One needs to be careful when reading material regarding proper breathing which uses the term diaphragmatic breathing. Many authors refer to abdominal breathing and/or thoracic breathing as diaphragmatic breathing. Since the diaphragm is the primary muscle used in breathing, regardless of what area we are using, those authors are correct. It is also possible to utilize other areas in addition to the lower thoracic/abdominal area when you are working out or running. And there is nothing wrong with that. My concern is that you work to maintain the lower thoracic/abdominal area as your habitual area for respiration or generating air pressure for speech.

Generally speaking, the length of time required for an inhale and an exhale for respiration are the same. But it is also okay to take short inhales and long exhales and vice versa. Speech requires a rapid inhale and a much slower exhale.

If you want to practice controlling your breathing speed, here is a good exercise. Take five seconds and do an inhale. Use another five seconds to complete the cycle with the exhale. Practice until this is easy to do. Now go to ten seconds for each half of the cycle. Keep practicing until you are comfortable. Now go for fifteen seconds. Continue at five-second intervals and work your way up to thirty seconds for each inhale and thirty seconds for each exhale. This really does take discipline but it can be very relaxing and invigorating. This exercise should also give you a great appreciation for the miracle of respiration and more control over how and when you choose to breathe.

Establishing the habit of good breath support and posture can be accomplished with consistent use of the following pattern: **Practice good posture, relax your neck and**

**shoulder muscles, and take cleansing breaths two to five minutes every hour for every hour you are awake for the rest of your life.** Get into the habit! As you practice, expand the two to five minute time span to four to eight minutes, then seven to ten minutes, and so on.

While you are doing "The Big Three" you should also practice counting to ten or reading the newspaper in the good voice quality. Whatever behavior you may be working to change or improve, get into the habit of practicing it. Watch your improvement over time. Use little reminders to always encourage you to "check yourself." Put a red dot on the face of your wrist watch as a subconscious reminder to straighten your posture, relax your neck and shoulder muscles, and to breathe using lots of cleansing breaths.

## THE PHONATORY SYSTEM: SOUND COMES FROM WHERE?

When the brain sends the message for speech to begin, air pressure is increased. The vocal folds are separated when the air is forced between them, and the folds begin to vibrate. The elasticity of the vocal folds allows them to stretch, and the muscles within the vocal folds remain tight, allowing them to continue vibrating. As air rushes through the vocal folds, a low-pressure area is created between them, which also helps keep the vocal folds pulled together.

The vocal folds are considered the primary source of vibration for the sounds of speech, but the articulators serve as a secondary source of vibration (see Figure 8.3). These articulators respond to the friction of air passing through the oral cavity. The lips, teeth, tongue, hard and soft palates, cheeks, and the alveolar ridge (the gum ridge above and in back of the upper front teeth) must all be in the appropriate position and serve as vibrators to add noise to sounds and also to

**Figure 8.3**

# Phonatory Systems

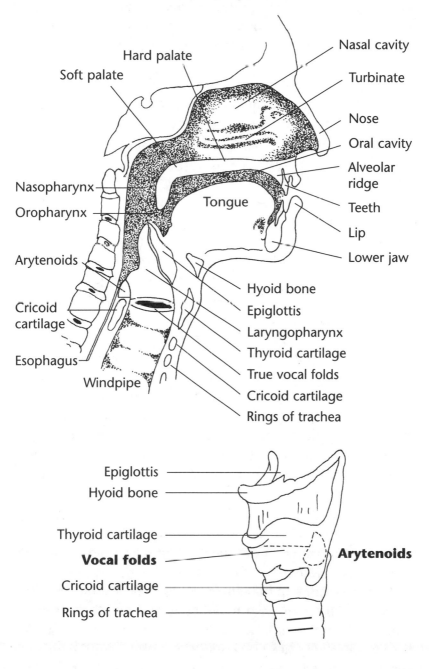

Hard palate

Soft palate

Nasal cavity

Turbinate

Nose

Oral cavity

Alveolar ridge

Nasopharynx

Oropharynx

Tongue

Teeth

Lip

Arytenoids

Lower jaw

Cricoid cartilage

Hyoid bone

Epiglottis

Laryngopharynx

Thyroid cartilage

Esophagus

True vocal folds

Windpipe

Cricoid cartilage

Rings of trachea

Epiglottis

Hyoid bone

Thyroid cartilage

**Vocal folds**

**Arytenoids**

Cricoid cartilage

Rings of trachea

shape them. For example, if I make a /z/ sound, I can feel the vibrations in my throat or larynx. I can also feel the vibrations of the front portion of my tongue against the alveolar ridge and the tongue tip against my lower front teeth.

As we discuss the various components of vocal delivery, we can improve the quality of our voices by knowing something about our vocal mechanism and how it works. To begin, we'll discuss the larynx, or the vocal process, and the most obvious part of the larynx, the thyroid cartilage, which is the largest cartilage of the vocal process. The thyroid cartilage is commonly known as the Adam's apple, that protrusion on the front of your neck.

To better understand the anatomy of the larynx, let's create a simple model using your hands. Place the heels of your hands together and cup the fingers of both hands so that the tips of the nails of all your fingers touch. Imagine the thyroid cartilage as starting from the second knuckle back from the tip of your index finger and going around the heels of your hands to the second knuckle of your other index finger.

This hand model will also give you a rough model of the vocal process. The hyoid bone can be imagined by visualizing a horseshoe-shaped bone a few inches above your thyroid cartilage. The shape would be similar to that made by you opening one hand with the tip of your thumb and index finger several inches apart and held above the thyroid cartilage model. The hyoid bone is the only bone in the vocal process and is open toward the rear, just like the thyroid cartilage. The hyoid bone is the suspension system for the rest of the vocal process. Muscles from the skull and jaw hold the hyoid bone in place. Muscles from the hyoid bone down to the thyroid cartilage hold up the remainder of the vocal process. You can actually feel your own hyoid bone by using the tips of your thumb and your index finger to grasp your neck immediately below your jaw bone. Raise your chin slightly and move your thumb and finger to the right and left gently. You should be able to feel your hyoid bone suspended from your lower jaw.

Back to the hand model of the vocal process. The fingernail section of your index fingers would be your arytenoid cartilages. These are in reality very small, pyramid-shaped cartilages which are capable of abducting and adducting, or opening and closing, the vocal folds and changing the length of the vocal folds. They accomplish this by rolling in their ball-and-socket-type connections on the superior, or top, surface, of the cricoid cartilage. (The term *superior* refers to direction, not to quality). Using the hands model, your index fingertips (arytenoids), would be rotating forward/back and separating right/left on the tips of your long fingers (your middle fingers), or the top surface of the cricoid cartilage.

To illustrate the cricoid cartilage and the rings of the trachea, rest your cupped hands around the top of a drinking glass with the tips of your long fingers and the base of your thumbs at the middle of your wrist on the top of the glass (see Figure 8.4). The cricoid cartilage completely encircles the vocal process. The hyoid and thyroid are open to the back,

**Figure 8.4**

# Hand Model

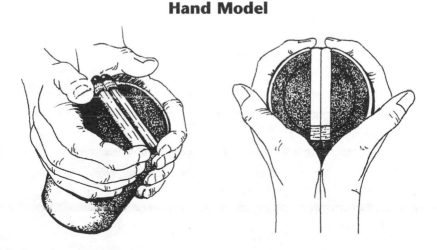

but the cricoid cartilage isn't. It is a complete ring, the only one in the vocal process. In the front, the cricoid cartilage is narrow and is below the thyroid cartilage—in your model, the heel of your hands. But the cricoid cartilage is wider in the back and rises to support the arytenoid cartilages.

The rings of trachea are also horseshoe-shaped cartilages that give shape to the windpipe. Imagine a series of thumb and index finger horseshoe-shaped cartilages around the glass you are using in your hands model. These rings are also open toward the back.

Now, the hyoid bone has been identified opening away from you hovering above the hands model. The large thyroid cartilage is facing you in your hands model, which is also open away from you. The cricoid cartilage completely surrounds the glass in the hands model, along with the rings of trachea. It's now time to place the vocal folds in our model.

Place two short pencils on top of the glass so that the eraser ends are together between the heels of your hands. They will represent the anterior connection of the vocal folds to the thyroid cartilage. The pencils should be just long enough to go all the way across the top of the glass. Then position the pencils against the tips of your index fingers, which represent the arytenoid cartilages, the posterior connection.

Because muscle names are generally taken from where they are attached, the vocal folds are called the thyroarytenoid muscles. The origin of the muscle is at the thyroid cartilage, while the insertion end is at the arytenoid cartilages. Now, by pulling your index fingers back and forth in the model, you can get a rough approximation of the vocal folds opening and closing.

When the vocal folds are abducted (pulled apart), the index fingers are pulled back. This positioning would allow you to be free to breathe. However, when you are speaking, the vocal folds are adducted (pulled together). Place your index fingers together so the pencils come together along their full lengths. This frees the vocal folds to vibrate along their full length. The hands model is relatively large. In reality, the vocal folds are about $^{3}/_{4}$-inch long in women and about one-inch long in men.

Keeping your thumbs together and bending them down over the pencils will allow them to operate as the epiglottis. This is the cartilage whose name means "cover of the glottis." The glottis is the space between or immediately beneath the vocal folds. Your thumbs are now able to completely cover the space and the vocal folds by folding down on top of the opening. The complex muscle structure within our vocal process allows for a much more sophisticated closure than our hand model can provide, but this model helps to give you an idea.

To expand our use of the model, to help you understand the complexity of this part of the anatomy, let's go through the process of taking a drink of water. The first mouthful of water is contained in the mouth—the oral cavity—by closing the soft palate against the back of the tongue, and the lips are closed. In the next step of the swallow, the soft palate closes against the back wall of the pharynx, closing off the nasal cavity. The oral cavity is opened so the liquid is free to move down the throat. At the same time, the vocal process is raised and pulled up underneath the muscles at the back of the tongue. In doing so, the epiglottis is lowered over the top of the vocal process and the back of the tongue is lowered. The closure of the vocal process is finished, allowing water to be muscled back and down into the esophagus. The esophagus is the food tube leading to your stomach whose top opening is just in back of the larynx. This muscle sheath begins posterior to the arytenoid cartilages. On the hands model, that would be in back of where the tips of the index fingers are located. The esophagus is in back of, or posterior to, the windpipe.

The esophagus takes swallowed items down to (or up from) the stomach. The esophagus is really a sheath of muscles that actually "muscles" items up or down. The muscle action is much like a snake swallowing its prey. In the swallow, the trip down the esophagus doesn't happen as shown in TV commercials where the pill bounces from one side to another in a big open tube and finally splashes into the stomach. We don't have many open cavities in our bodies like the nasal cavity and the vocal process. Most of those open spaces are filled with muscle tissue like our tongue in the oral cavity when we close our lips.

There you have it—your own model of the larynx. It is not intended to give you all the details but rather an overview of what is going on inside that structure in your neck.

## THE RESONATORY SYSTEM: SOUNDS LIKE AN ECHO!

Your body contains three resonating cavities used in speech: the *pharyngeal cavity,* the *nasal cavity,* and the *oral cavity* (see Figure 8.5). These resonating cavities amplify and augment the intensity of tone. In back of (posterior to) the epiglottis and above the vocal folds, when the vocal process is being used for breathing or speaking, is the lower portion of a space called the pharynx, or pharyngeal cavity. The pharynx is a resonating cavity that runs from above the vocal folds up past the back of the tongue to the back of the soft palate. It is arbitrarily broken into three areas. The lowest part of the larynx is called the *laryngopharynx* because it is located in the larynx. The pharyngeal space located at the back of the oral cavity is called the *oropharynx.* The third area is the space in back of the soft palate called the *nasopharynx.*

The soft palate is important in determining where sound is resonated. Changing the position of the soft palate obviously

**Figure 8.5**

# Resonatory Systems

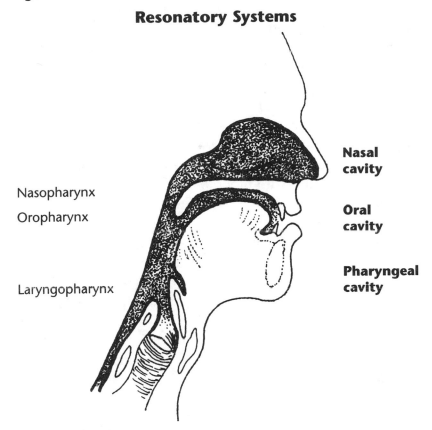

Nasopharynx

Oropharynx

Laryngopharynx

**Nasal cavity**

**Oral cavity**

**Pharyngeal cavity**

affects the size and shape of the nasopharynx. But the position of the soft palate has the greatest impact on how much the nasal cavity and/or oral cavity are utilized as resonators. When the soft palate is all the way down against the back of the tongue, the oral cavity is shut off and the sound is forced up into and is resonated in the nasal cavity. When the soft palate is all the way up and back against the pharyngeal wall, the resonated sound never enters the nasal cavity and is identified as being denasal. The quality of the resonated sound can be affected by obstructions in the nasal cavity.

The turbinates are bony structures in the nasal cavity that act as buffers, changing the direction of the air flow and adjusting the temperature of and cleansing incoming air. Often, excessive folds in the membranes of the nasal cavity or irregular muscle attachment to the soft palate can impede or encourage the use of the nasal cavity as a resonator. Problems resulting from obstructions vary depending on the condition. Air flow out of only one nostril, no air flow out of the nose at all, and an inability to stop air flow out of the nose as a person speaks are all indications of an obstruction or inefficiency. Also, trouble with pronouncing words may be an indication of an obstruction or physical problem. Someone may have large tonsils that restrict air flow and make efficient tongue movement difficult. Oversized or infected palatine tonsils and adenoids can cause a problem by affecting the size of the resonating cavity. A soft palate that is too long or too short can inhibit the ability to pronounce words also. Misshapen teeth can also affect articulation. The otolaryngologist is the specialist who can help determine the efficiency of the opening and closing of the soft palate and whether obstructions are impeding air flow in any of the resonating cavities.

## THE ARTICULATORY SYSTEM:
## BUT MY LIPS ARE MOVING!

Most often, an inability to produce intelligible speech depends on how the articulators are used. The articulators are the tongue, hard palate, soft palate, alveolar ridge, lips, and teeth (see Figure 8.6). The jaw is also included because of the movement it must make to move the teeth into position. For the production of most vowels, the top and bottom teeth need to be close to flush when the mouth is closed for the most proficient production.

**Figure 8.6**

# Articulatory Systems

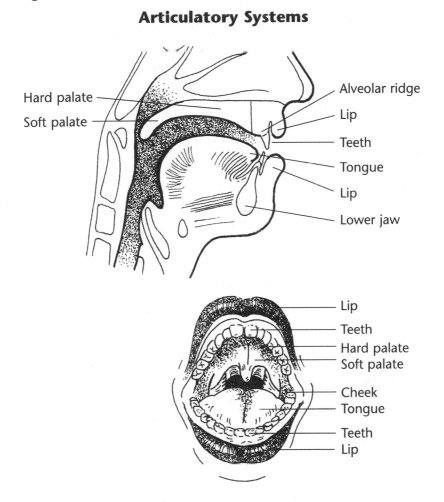

Hard palate

Soft palate

Alveolar ridge

Lip

Teeth

Tongue

Lip

Lower jaw

Lip

Teeth

Hard palate

Soft palate

Cheek

Tongue

Teeth

Lip

## Ear Training to Hear the Sounds Our Articulators Are Producing

The first part of our discussion on vocal delivery will focus on the ability to hear certain vocal behaviors and patterns in ourselves and other people. To do this, we will need to train our ears. Once we can hear the articulation choices we have available we can enunciate them or make decisions about how to use the articulators. Before we get into that training, let's go back to the basics and first become familiar with sound.

### The Nature of Sound: Three Characteristics

A force (air pressure) causes a source of sound (vocal folds) to vibrate, move back and forth. Technically, air molecules are moved forward and back at the number of times (a wave cycle) per second equal to the frequency of the vibrating source. Frequency is the physically measurable characteristic of vibration; pitch is how we label the perception of that vibration.

To sing or talk louder, we must vary the force or the strength of the energy (more or less air pressure) of the sound produced, changing its amplitude or intensity (the amount of movement of molecules forward and back). Amplitude or intensity is a second characteristic of vibration. Volume is how we label the perception of that characteristic. There is a third characteristic of vibration called spectrum, which deals with the configuration of a complex wave caused by characteristics of the vibrating source (density and mass). Most of us are aware of that characteristic as it applies to resonating elements, and we hear it as voice quality. As we discussed earlier, the voice qualities generally overshadow any other vocal fold (source of sound) characteristics.

## How We Hear: Three Stages

The next part of our discussion on vocal ability will focus on how we hear sound. Hilda Fischer identifies three stages in the hearing process. The first stage begins when successive sound waves (heard as one sound) enter the outer ear and push against the ear drum in the middle ear causing it to vibrate at the sound's frequency. A chain of tiny bones transmits the vibration from the ear drum to fluid inside the cochlea, a bony housing for the auditory nerve endings in the inner ear. The second stage in the hearing process is the perception of sound in the brain. When the small nerve endings in the cochlea are excited, nerve impulses are transmitted via the eighth nerve to the brain. The third step in hearing is auditory association. Incoming nerve impulses are perceived or identified and compared with the sounds a person has heard before. For most adults, there are very few sounds we haven't heard before. Once a sound is identified, it is labeled, categorized, stored, and used for reference the next time we hear that sound.

A brief example will illustrate how the sounds are categorized. Different guns make different and very distinctive noises when they are fired. If we are aware of those sound differences, we are free to discriminate and label them as we hear them. The twelve-gauge shotgun sounds differently than the twenty-two rifle. Both are distinct from either a thirty-eight or a forty-five pistol. If we are totally unfamiliar with the sounds made by the firing of weapons, then these sounds will be matched up with other similar loud noises. Other loud noises could be firecrackers or the back-firing of automobiles. We might "lump" these loud cracking sounds with the sounds of tree limbs breaking in a storm. We will use our previous sound memory bank to identify and match any new sounds.

If we are interested in changing or improving how we sound, we train our brain to utilize the feedback loop. First, we do the **inspection** of our sound production, with the help of a coach, by bringing it to our conscious level and examining it. Second, we do the **comparison** of our habitual sound with the desired sound until we can control turning both of them on and off as desired. Third, we do **correction** of the desired sound and continue practicing. Finally, **precorrection** takes over and those elements have been preset into the feedforward system. Those habit patterns become what we do when we are on automatic pilot.

## Problems With Automatic Pilot: Slipping into Cluelessness

This new habit joins others that keep our pronunciation of words, our dialect patterns, and movements consistent so that our brain is free to focus on the content of the messages. Our feedforward system checks all elements: rate, pitch, volume, voice qualities, air support, breathing, and muscle tension. Our habit behaviors are checked against our sense input as we experience those behaviors. Some of us train ourselves to consciously ignore information that is in conflict with our habit pattern. After time passes, that conscious ignoring also becomes unconscious and part of the automatic pilot program. As we get older, we can become less sensitive to our sensory input (due to hearing loss) and tend not to check those elements that are part of our speech output. Whether ignoring it or just getting older, we tend to assume that our speech is fine, and we give it little conscious thought. In reality, we are unaware of most of our speech output and its impact. We simply aren't attending to it.

## Steps for Using Our Senses for Self-Evaluation

In order to utilize the best intentions we may have regarding the use of the feedback loop, we must first awaken our capacity for sense input: seeing, feeling, hearing as they relate to speech production. Quite often we will be told by persons close to us that we have certain mannerisms when we talk, such as licking our lips or saying "uh," "like," or "you know" every few words. Most of us have a hard time believing someone when they tell us that. What this means is that although our senses are involved by collecting data at the subconscious level, our brains aren't doing anything with the feedback information. Where does this "come into play" for speakers? How about practicing to deliver a speech by standing in front of a mirror, but never seeing or feeling the muscles of our necks tighten? Or what about watching ourselves on videotape and never seeing that we speak out of one corner of our mouths, or not realizing that our lips don't move much when we speak?

The muscles are sending feedback to our brains, but we have not trained our brains to attend to that data. We have assumed that what we're doing is appropriate. Therefore, we don't see, feel, or hear the sound differences produced by that extra muscle activity or lack of it. How about hearing a lip smack at the ends of phrases or sentences, especially if we happen to be eating while we're talking or dropping the ends of words by not saying the voiced sounds like /d/ or /z/ at the ends of them? When people don't hear themselves doing this, it can be irritating. In order to respond to the feedback that is being sent to the brain, we need to do a few things.

First, we have to recognize that other people are concerned about how we sound. Utilize the feedback loop and do the inspection. Then, slow down, exaggerate, and repeat the troublesome sounds or distracting behaviors so that we are able to hear ourselves. But we'll need someone coaching us through this process. It also calls for us to put our hands on our faces, necks, and shoulders to know for sure what's moving and what isn't. It means identifying others who speak as we would like to and listening/watching as they produce individual sounds. It means listening to how they phrase ideas and the way they deal with volume, rate, voice qualities, and pitch. It also entails watching them and touching their faces and necks so we can see and feel the muscles they use or don't use as they speak. Then it is necessary to take all that information and imitate their speaking behaviors as if they were our own. Teaming up with someone, as mentioned, before, can be most helpful and is really mandatory if we desire permanent change.

I work with many clients who know they have a problem with keeping the sound in the back of the mouth. I thoroughly explain the problem so that they are aware of it intellectually. They are pulling their tongues back and articulating the sound in the back of their mouths. I exaggerate their problem by using negative practice contrast, imitating their voice qualities and how they sound to me. I demonstrate how I would like them to produce sound. They intellectually understand the problem; they can hear, see, and feel me imitating them and how I would like for them to produce sound. But they still can't get the kinesthetic feel for how it should be done. Finally, I place their hands on both sides of my face as I imitate how they produce sound and then move the sound forward, like I want them to produce it. Quickly, they get the feel for what has to be changed and moved so that they can duplicate my two exaggerated conditions. This is negative practice. They use their hands on their faces to get the kinesthetic feeling and resensitize their face muscles to transmit that data to the brain. They are now ready for the correction step. It may sound odd, but it works.

Let's give more detail to this process. Let's say you have a lazy lip; its movement is limited while you speak. Basically, you don't move the muscles of your upper lip when you speak. After some discussion, you understand intellectually the voice quality you are producing when you speak (muffled). You have done the step. You indicate that you can hear and see the changes made when I exaggerate my upper lip movement and when I don't. But when you exaggerate lip movement, there isn't any change. You think your upper lip is moving, but by looking in the mirror, we can both see that it isn't moving. Then you put the tips of two fingers on my upper lip to feel the exaggerated movement of my upper lip as I count to 10. Again, I let you feel the lack of movement, as I count to 10 with the sound articulated in the back of my mouth. It is very easy for you to put two fingers on your upper lip to reproduce the movement or lack of it as you count to 10.

Voice training is really the process of training your ear to hear sound differences. Once trained, your ear can help you discriminate between sounds. But that's not all there is to it. In order to get your ear trained so that you can fine tune your communication behaviors, you must utilize your other sensory input. Communication behavior is learned. Most of the time people are unaware of the decisions they've made regarding their communication behaviors. They didn't realize they had choices. Once you become aware of the choices, you can make conscious decisions based on what you know, rather than going with those previous decisions when you have lacked adequate information. The more you know, the more choices you have and you should be better equipped to adapt your communication behavior to people, situations, and the communication task at hand. Correcting the positioning of your articulators can best be accomplished by being aware of the production of each of the sounds and the impact of voice quality change.

# THE SOUNDS YOUR VOICE PRODUCES

## IPA: THE SOUNDS OF OUR LANGUAGE

Phonetics is the study of the sounds of a spoken language. The International Phonetic Alphabet (IPA) can be helpful because it provides a symbol or a pair of symbols for each sound or sound combination that we use in our language. Knowing the symbols and their sounds allows you to identify sound production errors you may be making.

When we produce sounds, people may not hear our words as we intended them to sound. Too often, we don't even realize that we are not producing the sound in an acceptable, precise manner. Sometimes, when we do realize that we are incorrectly producing a sound, we try to hide it or overuse it; we also have a tendency to joke about it and often worry about it. Luckily, our language is redundant enough that if only a few sounds are produced incorrectly, it won't matter in the long run. But if we habitually "mess up" in saying the sounds of our language, people will perceive us as less than we really are.

Memorizing the IPA system of symbols is a good idea. It will often help your spelling. But most important, it makes changing the way you produce certain sounds much easier.

For example, one southern sound combination that gets attention and a laugh is saying the word *that* with an extra vowel after the *a*. The added vowel sounds like *uh*. So the word *that* becomes *tha-uh-t*. If we hear others say "tha-uh-t," we can transcribe their production of the word in IPA. Then we can compare this incorrect production of *that* to its correct production. This provides a model you can use to compare your own production of certain words.

Using IPA helps us to say names or words we may not be able to say properly because of how they look when they are written. If a coworker or client gave his or her name to you over the phone and it was an unusual, hard-to-pronounce name, how would you remember it a few days from now? Many of us would guess at its spelling when we wrote it down and hope this was close to correct. We often write the name down as we heard the person saying it. And we hope that when we read it later, how we've written it will allow us to pronounce it correctly. If we are good with names or have a good memory, we might be able to recall that pronunciation a few days later. If we see the "strange" name written out, we may not make the connection with how we had hoped to say it. But with the IPA skills available to us, we can write down the sounds in the name and repeat them back exactly as we heard them. We can do this because we've learned a system of sounds that accounts for all the sounds in our language. Talk about a strategy for making friends and influencing people! Being able to pronounce a difficult name and being able to do it consistently after hearing it only once is very impressive.

Basically, there are two strategies available for learning the sounds and symbols of the IPA. The first strategy is to take similar sounds in clusters and gain mastery of those sounds and symbols before moving on to the next cluster. This process could take weeks. Lots of transcription focusing on the target cluster would be involved. It is a lot like learning to swim: During the first lesson, we get our feet wet; for the next lesson, we may end up getting waist-deep into the water; and for the third lesson, we get our whole body wet and try to float. And the step-by-step lessons go on.

The second strategy for learning IPA is to go over all the sounds and symbols in a quick overview and then practice transcription using all the sounds and symbols until a level of mastery has been attained. Using the learning-to-swim analogy, this strategy involves a quick overview of the basics and then walking to the end of the diving board and jumping into the deep end of the pool. Yes, there would be lots of lifeguards available when those first jumps are made!

We will be using the second approach to learning the symbols and sounds of IPA. Learning these symbols may be overwhelming, but don't give up. Keep practicing. As you practice more, IPA will become second nature to you. You may even find yourself writing in IPA when you really mean to write just plain English! We will begin with a discussion of some of the basics and several of the potential problems.

Some IPA basics are necessary before we even get near the water. Sounds in our language fall into several categories. One of those categories is voicing. If the vocal folds are generating vibration, the sound we are producing is voiced. If the vocal folds are not vibrating when the sound is produced, the sound is voiceless. You can feel that vibration, or lack of it, by putting your hand on the front of your throat and saying a pair of sounds. We call pairs of sounds produced alike that differ only in voicing cognates. Let's use the lips to say /b/, the voiced sound, and /p/, the voiceless sound. Can you feel the vibration difference? Can you hear the difference? Another IPA basic is the difference between consonants and vowels. Vowels are made by changing the hump in your tongue while keeping the tip of your tongue next to your lower front teeth (see Appendix B). We learned in elementary school that there were only six vowels: *a, e, i, o,* and *u* (and sometimes *y*). But we also learned that those six vowels were responsible for a lot more sounds; some vowel sounds are short ones and some are long ones. Check your dictionary for a list of vowel variations. In IPA, there are individual symbols for each of those different sounds. We will talk about those vowel differences later.

Consonants provide a whole array of different configurations in production, duration, and resonance. Within the consonants, there are five general classifications to make sound identification easier. There are stop consonants, fricatives, affricates, glides/semivowels, and nasals. There are six stop consonants, or stop plosives. For these six sounds, the vocal tract is closed at the point of constriction, air pressure builds, and then the air pressure is released in an explosive puff of air. The air is pushed over the center of the tongue. There are three cognate pairs of stop plosives. As cognates, sounds that differ only in voicing, both are practiced with the same articulator configuration and air pressure. You will notice that voiceless sounds appear to require more air and the voiced sounds require more effort to maintain the vibration.

The /p/–/b/ are produced at the lips. To make these sounds, close the lips, build air pressure, then explode open the lips. The sound is produced quickly and only once with that burst of air. To make the sound again, one must repeat the process; the sound is not continuous or ongoing. The voiceless /p/ appears in words such as *paid, weeping,* and *soup.* The voiced /b/ appears in words such as *beat, obey,* and *job.* Can you hear and feel the vibration differences as you produce these words? To make the differences easier to detect, replace the /p/ for the /b/ in the example words and say them again. Changing the voicing for a sound in a word can change the meaning dramatically. These new words may be nonsense words, but they allow you to hear and experience the differences in sound production.

The /t/–/d/ are produced by putting the tip of the tongue against the alveolar ridge, building air pressure, then dropping the tongue for the production of the sound. The voiceless /t/ appears in words such as *till, written,* and *late.* The voiced /d/ appears in words such as *den, maiden,* and *bad.* Again, practice saying the sounds out loud and listen for the voiced and voiceless /t/ and /d/.

The last pair of stop plosives, /k/–/g/, are produced when the back of the tongue is raised and closes against the soft palate. The voiceless /k/ appears in words such as *key, rake,* and *lock.* The voiced /g/ appears in words such as *go, begin,* and *plug.* Be sure that you practice these sounds so that you can hear the differences. If you need to, switch the sounds in the example words and say the nonsense words.

To review, the stop consonants are made by completely closing off the vocal tract at a point of constriction. This can be at either the lips, the alveolar ridge, or the soft palate while the air pressure continues to build. Then suddenly, that particular area is reopened for a single explosion to produce the sound.

The other four classifications of consonants are all known as continuants. In contrast to the very quick stop plosives, the continuants can keep sound going on over time. The only restriction to producing these sounds continually is your ability to sustain the air pressure necessary to produce the sound.

The largest group of continuants is made up by the nine sounds classified as fricatives. The term *fricative* implies that these sounds require some constriction in the oral tract in addition to vocal fold vibration. The sounds can be elongated and produced for as long as you have air pressure to sustain the sound.

The /s/ sound poses production problems for many people. The /s/ sound and the /z/ sound are produced by pointing the tip of the tongue at the base of the lower front teeth and humping the middle part of the tongue up against the alveolar ridge. This restricts the air flow across the center of the tongue. Just where you place the tip of your tongue in your mouth is up to you. But remember that the clearest /s/–/z/ sounds are produced when the middle of the tongue creates the constriction at the alveolar ridge and the tip of the tongue is on or close to the lower teeth. The /s/ sound is easiest to produce once the tongue is in position by raising the corners of the upper lip slightly, restricting air from flowing out the edges of the mouth on either side of your tongue. To make the /z/ sound, position your articulators as you would to make the /s/ sound and simply voice the sound (cause the vocal folds to vibrate).

Many people who produce the /s/ sound in a noisy manner with air coming out over the top of the tongue and even out the edges of the mouth just never learned how to produce it correctly. Those noisy /s/ sounds really raise havoc when microphones are involved. The sound is amplified and distorted, often requiring screens or deflection devices mounted on the microphones or electronic filters built into the system. Several conditions can contribute to a noisy /s/. It's either the placement of the tip of the tongue or the inappropriate positioning of the teeth. Let's deal with positioning of the teeth first. Some speakers never (or rarely) move their lower jaws forward so that their front teeth approximate. If the front teeth are flush or close to flush during the production of the /s/, the sound will be clearer. Try pulling your lower jaw back slightly as you raise your lower jaw. With your lower teeth in back of your upper teeth try producing a clear /s/ sound. Now while you are still producing the /s/ sound move your lower jaw slowly forward until the lower teeth are flush with your upper teeth. As you continue with the /s/ move your lower jaw (teeth) past your upper teeth. You should hear lots of air passing producing a noisy /s/ sound when your lower jaw is behind or extended out in front of your upper teeth. The quietest /s/ sound production should occur as your teeth are closest to flush. Be sure to practice this out loud. Several choices are available for where to position the tip of your tongue as you produce the /s/ sound.

Those tongue-tip positions vary from your alveolar ridge down to below the gum line on your lower teeth. I recommend trying to keep your tongue tip against the back of your lower front teeth. This position generally results in the cleanest and quietest /s/ sound production.

There are several reasons for this. The /s/ sound point of articulation is between the muscles of the tongue and the alveolar ridge. Speakers often produce the /s/ by blowing air between the closed teeth while completely disregarding the position of the tongue. This results in a very noisy /s/ sound production. In order to accomplish the appropriate tongue position for the desired sound, the tongue tip must be close to the lower teeth with the hump of the tongue pushed up against the alveolar ridge. In that position, the tongue is in the best position possible to create the friction necessary for a clear /s/ sound. If the tongue tip is placed at the gum ridge of the upper teeth or higher, the tongue tip is raised as the friction point for the /s/ sound. The tongue tip does not make very complete closure and lots of air is allowed to escape.

The muscles of the lips are generally contracted slightly, pulled up and back, to produce the clearest /s/ and /z/ sound possible. The correctly produced /s/ and /z/ are quieter than when the air is escaping less efficiently.

Some people may have trouble fading on the /z/ sound. Fading is the lowering of pitch and volume on the ends of words, particularly those that come at the ends of phrases and sentences. Those who rarely voice the /z/ sound, particularly at the ends of words, generally fade the ends of /z/

words in an attempt to compensate for that exclusion. How do you say "ends of words"? Do you end those two /z/ words with /ts/ or /dz/? People who fade the /z/ sound also do so because it allows them to diminish the impact of their noisy /z/ sound. If they drop pitch and volume on that sound, maybe no one will notice the extra noise.

The next two fricatives are the *th* sounds. They are easily produced if you simply put your tongue between the teeth, bite down slightly, and blow air over the top and center of the tongue. You can check to see if your tongue is in the correct position by placing your index finger on your lips as if signaling someone to be quiet as you produce the *th* sounds; the tip of your tongue should touch your finger. The constriction is over the tongue and the upper front teeth. Too many people don't put their tongues between the teeth, but rather up against the upper front teeth or the alveolar ridge. Instead of saying *this* and *that,* they produce *dis* and *dat.* The voiceless *th,* /θ/, appears in words such as <u>th</u>in, <u>th</u>ink, and bo<u>th</u>. The voiced *th,* /ð/, appears in words such as <u>th</u>at, <u>th</u>is, and ba<u>th</u>e.

Another pair of fricatives, the /v/ and /f/, are made by pulling the top portion of the lower lip between the teeth and blowing air over the lip. The constriction is over the lower lip and the upper front teeth. Instead of pulling the lower lip between their teeth, many people pull the back part of the lip between their teeth or use their tongue tip to fill the gap. All too often, the words that end in the /v/ sound are faded so the /f/ is produced instead. *Five* then becomes *fife.* The /v/ voiced sound appears in words such as *vi<u>v</u>id, fi<u>v</u>e,* and *ali<u>v</u>e.* The voiceless /f/ sound appears in words such as *<u>f</u>it, buffet,* and *duff.* Hearing a respected news anchor say he "works for Channel Fife News" is very distracting.

Not as frequently used are two more cognate fricatives. These are the voiced and voiceless *sh,* /ʒ/ and /ʃ/. The tongue is held high in your mouth with the tip just in back of the alveolar ridge. The constriction of air occurs where the middle of the tongue very lightly meets the roof of the mouth and forces the air to hit the tips of the lower front teeth. You should purse the lips forward as if you were putting your index finger to your lips to say "sh" to a loud talker. The voiceless *sh*, /ʃ/, appears in words such as *sheep, brushes*, and *rush*. The voiced *sh*, /ʒ/, appears in the words *Za Za* (Gabor), *leisure, treasure*, and *evasion*.

The last fricative is the voiceless /h/ as in *help*. The constriction is between the vocal folds. The /h/ appears in words such as *how, had*, and *who*.

There are nine fricatives in all: /s/, /z/, /θ/, /ð/, /f/, /v/, /ʒ/, /ʃ/, and /h/. All use a manner of production that requires secondary friction or vibration in addition to the voiced vocal folds. You can produce each of these sounds as long as you have air pressure to sustain the sound.

Sometimes fricatives and stop plosives are combined. There are a couple of sounds in our language that are produced in this way. By combining a plosive /t/ or /d/ with a fricative /ʃ/ or /ʒ/ respectively, the resulting combination produces sounds called affricates. The /tʃ/ combination is the *ch* sound. It is voiceless and appears in the word *church*. The /dʒ/ combination is voiced, and it is the *g, j*, and *dg* sound, as in *judge*.

Three consonants are also fricatives, but they are further classified as nasal sounds, with the air being forced up and out through the nasal cavity. The resulting sound is determined by where the complete closure occurs. The /m/ sound is produced by closing the oral cavity and the lips while voicing the sound. Words such as *me, bomb*, and *lamb* contain the /m/ sound. The /n/ sound is produced by putting the tongue tip on the alveolar ridge and preventing air from escaping from the oral cavity. The /n/ sound can be found in the words *now, bunny*, and *span*. With the *ng* sound, /ŋ/, the tongue is raised to meet the soft palate. This closes off the oral passage and the sound is vibrated through the nasal cavity. When you say the word *sing* and hold the ending *ng* sound, you will notice the *g* is not the last sound. It is silent as in words such as *king*, and *singing*.

This leaves us with five more consonant sounds to discuss. The voiced and voiceless *w* are sometimes called glides, or semivowels, because the articulators are moving as the sounds are being produced. Technically, they cannot be produced in isolation. They need other vowel sounds in front or in back of them so that they are produced clearly. The air is forced near the center of the tongue. The back of the tongue is raised toward the soft palate and the lips are rounded as the articulators move to produce the vowel that follows. The voiced /w/ appears in words such as *watt, one, wait,* and *will*. The voiceless /ʍ/ appears in words such as *what, why, where, when, white, whiskers, whisper,* and *whether*. Using *watt* and *what* for negative practice can help you hear the difference. Sometimes we spell words using the *h* sound, as in *who, whose, whom,* and *whole*.

The /j/ sound is also a glide or semivowel. The air is forced over the center of the tongue. Again, the tongue is arched toward the hard palate, and the tongue is moving to produce the vowel that follows. The voiced sound /j/ appears in words such as *you, yellow,* and *young*.

The /r/ sound is also a glide or semivowel. Air is forced over the top of the tongue, the tip of which is raised slightly just in back of the alveolar ridge. The sides of the tongue in back should be touching the sides of the teeth. The voiced /r/ sound appears in words such as *run, rose, erase, very, near,* and *poor*. The /r/ sound best demonstrates the glide characteristics of a vowel sound. You can hear a clear, clean /r/ when saying the word *run*. But when trying to say an /r/ in isolation, it's impossible. The /r/ will sound more like an *er*, /ɚ/.

The final glide or semivowel to be discussed is the /l/ sound. In this sound, the air is forced over the sides of the tongue, laterally, because the tongue tip actually touches the alveolar ridge. The /l/ sound is voiced and appears in words such as *lip, allow,* and *swell.* On the /l/ sound, the back of the tongue is raised even higher and elongated for a "dark" /l/, as in *pillow* and *still.*

That concludes the consonant sounds in IPA. The most troublesome sounds for people are usually the voiced and voiceless *th,* the *f, v, d, t, s,* and *z* sounds, particularly in combinations. Many people have difficulty with combinations in words such as *asks, artists, fifth*—and the list goes on and on. Check the mispronunciation table at the end of this chapter.

As we mentioned previously, the IPA provides us with fifteen separate vowel sounds. Why are there so many? We use the *a, e, i, o, u* letters as such in lots of words, but there are lots of other sounds they are responsible for. In IPA, all of those many sounds have separate symbols. In addition, syllables that are unstressed require different vowel sounds. Combinations of vowel sounds, known as diphthongs, account for another half dozen symbols. Rather than indicating whether the vowel sound is short or long, phonemes (or sounds) are isolated and each is specified by a specific symbol.

We use all these vowel sounds in our language, but most of us don't hear the subtle differences among some of them. No one has called it to our attention since we simply don't discriminate. It is likely that we probably don't produce them correctly either. If we don't habitually make these distinctions, we won't sound as fluent or intelligent. As a result, our image and credibility suffers.

The vowels are all produced while keeping the tip of your tongue on or very close to your lower front teeth. Making changes in the hump of your tongue actually produces the vowel sound differences. Imagine the vowels appearing in a V shape on the side of your face. Start the V at the corner of your lips. Move back and down to the middle of your lower jaw, then back up a couple of inches toward your ear. Vowels produced up high and toward the front of that V are /i/ as in *see* and /ɪ/ as in *it*. Those lower down on the V are mid front middle vowels, such as /e/ as in the word *date*, /ɛ/ as in *bet*, and /æ/ as in *cat*. The low front vowels are /a/, as in *ice* and /ɑ/ as in *father*. The sounds on the back side of the V— toward your ear—are produced in the back of your mouth. The low back vowels are /ɒ/ as in *watch* and /ɔ/ as in *law*. The mid back vowel is /o/ as in *boat*. The high back vowels are /ʊ/ as in *book* and /u/ as in *boot*. The central vowels include the unstressed schwa /ə/ as in *sofa* and schwa-r /ɚ/ as in *after*. The schwa symbol allows us to account for the unstressed vowel sounds found in unstressed syllables. Also, included in the central vowels are the stressed phonemes /ɜ/ as in *thor-oughbred* (with the syllable break after the first *o*) or *button* (when raising the pitch slightly on the first syllable), /ɝ/ as in *hurt,* and lastly, the stressed /ʌ/ as in *up.*

There are four diphthongs within the IPA. They are: /ju/ as in *few,* /aɪ/ as in *I,* /aʊ/ as in *down,* and /ɔɪ/ as in *coin.* Other pairs of sounds treated as diphthongs are /jʊ/ as in *your* or *Europe,* /ɛr/ as in *air,* /eɪ/ as in *eight* (really exaggerated like a country southerner), and /oʊ/ as in *toad* or *boat* (really exaggerated again).

The IPA system is easy to understand intellectually, but you have to practice often to use the system correctly and automatically. Audiotape examples, flashcards, and working with a partner can be helpful. Audio- and videotapes are available from the author. IPA is effective to use when you have difficulty with certain sounds or words. A good practice to get into is to keep word lists. Look up words in the dictionary when you think you may mispronounce them. Many of us mispronounce words such as *library.* Some people say something that sounds like *lieberry.* Try writing those trouble-some words in IPA and check to see if you are producing all the sounds correctly. You may want to work on certain sounds, like the /s/ in *isolation,* for a bit and then try the word or words that you feel you need to work on.

Here are some of the best sources for additional information on the International Phonetic Alphabet.

Heinberg, Paul. *Voice Training for Speaking and Reading Aloud.* New York: Ronald Press, 1964.

Newcombe, P. Judson. 2nd ed. *Voice & Diction.* Raleigh: Contemporary Publishing, 1991.

Eisenson, Jon. 7th ed. *Voice and Diction: A Program for Improvement.* Boston: Allyn and Bacon, 1997.

Crannell, Kenneth C. *Voice and Articulation.* Belmont: Wadsworth, 1987.

## ARTICULATION, ENUNCIATION, AND PRONUNCIATION

The words *articulation, enunciation,* and *pronunciation* are often used interchangeably by authors writing about the voice. Other authors suggest that *articulation* refers to the production of consonant sounds, *enunciation* refers to vowel sound production, and *pronunciation* refers to uttering words or syllables. These differing terms can cause confusion among readers. To help you understand the terms and make them clearer, I have selectively narrowed the definitions of these terms to make them more distinctive.

Articulation is the movement or the positioning of the articulators to shape the sounds in the oral cavity clearly; this includes both consonants and vowels. Vowel production requires much less articulator movement because the tongue is always against the lower teeth; changing the hump in the tongue is the biggest movement required when producing vowel sounds. For consonants, it is quite a different story. Changes in the positioning of the lips, the tongue, and the soft palate are required.

Enunciation concerns an individual's decision about how to use the articulators to produce sound. Although an individual's speech patterns may be influenced by a particular culture or geographic region, how someone produces the sounds of a language is based on personal decisions. Sometimes, we have made the decision to say a word a certain way because that's how members of our culture chose to produce it. Other times, we make the decision to sound different from our culture for personal reasons.

As a voice coach, I am hired to work with individuals to help them make communication behavior changes which they deem appropriate. They have made the decision to change how they communicate. Yet many clients do not make the changes I am anticipating they will make. For example, I may have been trying to help them alleviate distorted consonant or vowel sounds. These are minor changes which a speech pathologist would not define as a problem. Even though these clients had made the decision to change they were not altering their behaviors. It appears the decisions were at two different levels. The "I need to change my communication to make it better" decision was easy for them to make. It was an intellectual thing. The "Gosh, I have to change these specific behaviors" wasn't as easy to accomplish. This decision calls for action and a lot of concentrated work. Sometimes this second decision was very conscious. These clients were up front with me. They simply were not going to do the work necessary to make the changes happen. Most of the time, my clients did not realize that they had made this second decision not to change their behaviors. This decision was masked behind a lot of negative statements. "I'm not sure I can do this." "This just doesn't sound like me." "No one will recognize me." "They will think I am putting on airs." "People don't talk like that where I'm from." "This is too difficult for me." And the list goes on. . . .

Rather than work with these clients on positioning their articulators for clarity, I had to concentrate on their attitude and what they were feeling regarding the specific changes required. Subconsciously, they had associated how they sounded with who they were. Changing how they sounded would impact who they were. The change would have more impact than they thought originally. Perhaps it is likely that they were combining their feelings of inadequacy in speaking with the value they were placing on their personal worth. Therefore, openly discussing communication inadequacies would be directly attaching who they saw they were (or weren't) on the inside. They weren't going to risk that confrontation even though they were paying for my time. And they continued on with the instruction, in spite of still making the decision not to change. A lot of us find ourselves in the same situation. We have to remember that how we sound is not who we are. Our audiences only see our behaviors. If we want to change how they perceive us then we must change our communication behaviors.

Pronunciation is the appropriateness or correctness of the way words, phrases, and sentences are said. Correctness is really determined by the preferences of our choice reference group. The majority of audiences available are still most easily reached when our pronunciation choices are consistent with standard English. The sources of that appropriateness could be dictionaries, radio and TV usage, the Internet, checking with other locals, or our own personal preferences.

In order to be pronouncing words as we have chosen to say them, the articulators need to be working appropriately. It is necessary that we make decisions about articulator use so that they are part of our habit pattern.

There are at least four steps in this word choice and usage process. First, we have an idea in our minds. We know the idea we want to share. Second, we choose words, phrases, and sentences that will carry the meaning we want to share. Third, our brains send orders to our articulators to say those sentences. The fourth step is actually saying those words.

Assume we are polished professional speakers. We have confidence in our well-trained feedforward system. We continually monitor it and update it. If that is all true then coming up with the idea is really the only part of the process that is done at the conscious level. All the rest of the process is handled primarily by our feedforward system. We may be thinking about it but most of the decisions have already been made. Our brain is ready to proceed. If we have involved ourselves in vocabulary building we will "automatically" choose the best words. If we have monitored our sound production, adjusted our delivery to the preferred pronunciation standard, and dealt with the enunciation decisions we'll "automatically" make the sounds to pronounce the words correctly. If we have monitored our posture, neck and shoulder muscle tension, breath support, movements, and gestures, we will "automatically" deliver our message with consistent credibility.

Let's assume that we have not reached a level of quality consistent with that of a polished professional speaker. When we have not prepared ourselves by raising our word choice and usage standards then we are not free to utilize our feedforward system for spontaneous delivery. That means we will be making conscious decisions at each of the four steps in the word choice and usage process. For many of us this is where communication apprehension becomes a reality. When we can't rely on our daily habits of word choice and usage then we have to make those decisions while on stage. Those decisions are now being made in real time rather than being pre-planned. That makes us nervous. Making those word choice and usage decisions takes more time to implement. As a result, we perceive ourselves as unsure and not very fluent. Our audiences agree with us. We personalize those perceptions. That makes us even more nervous. And the procedure goes on.

The question is not **if**, but rather **when** we choose to make those conscious word choice and usage decisions that is at issue. If we had started working on our word choice, pronunciation, and delivery patterns long ago we would be ready now. If and when a speaking opportunity became available our feedforward system would be available to use. The appropriate decisions would already have been made. As we persist in upgrading the quality of our vocabulary, pronunciation, and delivery, the quality of our decisions regarding our performances will improve.

Although word choice is not part of the focus/mission of this book, how those words are pronounced must be considered. Appropriate sound production, the unobtrusive use of vocal variables, and appropriate movement, however, are the focus of this book.

## PRONOUNCIATION VARIATIONS: DEPENDING ON THE SITUATION

I believe that how you pronounce words is your business. I also believe that there are no absolutely correct ways to pronounce most words in our language. A young friend of mine has the given name of Kenneth. When I met him, I tried to call him Ken. He corrected me and told me that his Mom calls him Kin (rhymes with thin). I can't argue with that.

Consider the name of an explorer that has been given to several towns in the United States: Lafayette. What community you are in will determine how you use the stress pattern to say the name of the town. Who can say which pronunciation is correct? How you pronounce words depends on your circumstances and the audience involved. How much you want other people to understand you is also a choice. Hence, the more standard the pronunciation you use, the more standard the response you will get from the audience with whom you desire to share meaning.

How successful you want your communication to be depends, in part, on how you pronounce those words. Just because you mispronounce a word does not mean that you are wrong. But those "observed mispronunciations" will have a lot to do with how others perceive you. Those who mispronounce words, or who say them differently from the standard of the group, are generally perceived as being less intelligent or less educated than the others in the group. Exceptions would be dialects such as British, Scottish, or Irish.

Many of us have struggled through the growing-up process with trying to keep everyone happy about how we used language. At home and at school, we were corrected on language usage or on how to say particular words. As we know, speech is a learned behavior. We learned our sound, voice quality, pitch, rate, volume, and pronunciation patterns from the first adults we encountered. We also learned our gestures and other delivery behaviors from these same adults.

The process continued when we began interacting with our peers. As we grew up, we sometimes made conscious decisions about changing what we said and how we would say it so that we would fit in. But most often, we made these changes subconsciously. We may have been trying to interact appropriately with the adults in our lives as well as with our peers. But sometimes, we failed to interact successfully because of our language use. We were probably trying to please one or both groups. The greater the language differences between the two groups, the greater the chances that pronunciation differences would appear. That is one source of mispronunciation of words.

Another source of mispronunciation comes from our use and misuse of dialects. When we leave the home of our familiar language use patterns and seek livelihood elsewhere, we interact with folks who use slightly different dialects. Generally speaking, the biggest difference between dialects is in how we choose to pronounce words. Few things make life as complicated as the perceptual differences created as we observe others communicating using dialect patterns different from ours. Even for those who are from the South, hearing a country southerner say *tha-uh-t* instead of *that* can be startling.

A third source of mispronunciation differences comes from being sloppy or negligent in our pronunciation. A few examples for you: *git* for *get, ain't* for *is not* or *are not,* and *jist* for *just.* If we are not carefully monitoring ourselves, comparing what we are really saying to how we are trying to say it, we may not even hear it. It's perfectly normal not to hear the differences. It is also normal for most of us to be sloppy in our language production. Good clear language production requires paying frequent attention.

A fourth source of mispronunciation derives from very specialized dialect patterns. These dialect patterns are shared by a group of people having something in common, sometimes in a specific regional area. Often referred to as "slangs," these dialects are used for shared communication among its users. Up to this point, these dialects are not different from any other dialect. But there are other additional purposes for the use of these slangs. Often, the reason for their use is to confuse or talk down to another group or set of individuals.

Two well-known examples of such dialects are ebonics and the valley-girl pattern, or valley speech. Ebonics is a form of dialect used by many in the African American culture. There are those who will argue that ebonics has been in use for over 200 years. Linguists may refer to ebonics as Black English or African American Vernacular English. Ebonics is also considered to have specific grammatical and linguistic rules. Some common characteristics of ebonics include using one verb form for all subjects, as in "I be goin," and variation in the production of the *th* sound, as in *mouf* (for mouth) and *dem* (for them).

While doing some informal research on ebonics, I questioned a large group of self-admitted users of ebonics. Most had learned it as children and some had not learned it until they were in high school or college. Most freely admitted that if they had a choice, they would not use it when the occasion called for or required clear, successful communication. They did use it to share greetings, engage in small talk, to "show off" to those around them, and to talk about someone, particularly if that person wasn't there.

The tragedy, for me, concerning the use of ebonics is that many ebonics users do not have a choice in communication strategies. They do not have a clear speech pattern available to them that is not distracting. If ebonics is their first and only language, there will be communication problems as they attempt to interact with members of other groups in our culture. The lack of understanding caused by the stereotypical perceptions imposed on these dialect users is too hard to overcome without other language choices available.

The "valley-girl" language pattern is so named because of its origin, the San Fernando Valley in California. Its wide use among the area's young citizens was made well known in the larger popular culture. Many comedy shows on television satirized this dialect pattern, with its high-pitched voices, rising pitch patterns, and constant use of the word *like,* as in "Do you, like, understand?"

The valley-girl speech pattern is in many ways similar to ebonics. And the same problems exist as with ebonics. Although valley speech was rather faddish and popular, recognition of it has somewhat passed. However, users of this dialect pattern may find that successful communication is limited.

The spin-off form of this dialect pattern is often called "up speak." Its key characteristic is a rise in pitch on the ends of words, phrases, and sentences. The stereotype perceptions that this dialect pattern generates almost always terminate successful communication with someone who does not use this pattern. It's okay to use any of these dialect patterns but you should use another dialect pattern when more meaningful communication is necessary.

How you pronounce words should really depend on who you are talking to, where you are, and your communication goals. Let's say your communication goal is to sell a product. If you learned your language in a specific dialect community, returning to that community for a sales call will require returning to usage of its dialect. However, if you use that very specific dialect in other communities where another dialect is prevalent, there may be communication problems. Your success as a communicator, your image of being competent, and your potential for achievement might be at risk.

At this point, we need a good, expensive example of how mispronounced words can impact your life. Recently, a student shared with me a very touching story directly related to how he says the *th* sound. He had gotten into the habit of saying the voiced or voiceless *th* sound by pulling the back of his lower lip up to his upper front teeth to generate the friction to make the sound. The voiceless *th* is more appropriately produced by putting the tongue between the teeth to get the sound friction over the top of the tongue and against the teeth. You guessed it. His production of the *th* sound was really a rather sloppy *f* sound. The name of his new girlfriend was Heather. He was in love. She was wonderful. He had called her by a lot of names, "honey," "sweetheart," and the like, but never by her given name. She had never heard him say it

before. Then, one evening, while out with a group of acquaintances, he introduced her. "I would like for you to meet my
honey, Heffer." It was as close to her given name as he could
get. But Heather is not the name they heard. They heard
Heifer. He said he is currently looking for a new girlfriend.

You can best utilize the word list in Table 9.1 by adding
words in which sounds are altered or omitted by your dialect
community. The list does not include all the examples I've
collected. However, I have tried to make sure most of the
sounds are dealt with.

Being consistent with the rules of IPA, I am putting the
stress marks in front of the syllable being stressed. For example, the word *happy* is often said with the first syllable stressed
and the second syllable unstressed. In IPA, the word is written
/'hæ pə/.

There are bound to be some of you who have never had
the opportunity to learn, let alone be aware of, the study of
syllables in our language. Syllables are those single sounds or
sound combinations that are clumped together to form
words. Some of these sound clumps are given more stress—in
other words, are made to be louder, to be elongated, or to
have a higher pitch. Any or all of these three variables may
be used to stress words in our language. Some words, such as
*go, see, man,* and *the,* have only one syllable. Others have two
or more syllables: *good-bye, he-llo, man-u-script.* (I am using the
hyphen (-) to indicate the break between syllables.)

I have put the list in alphabetic order, rather than by
sound type. I have listed the substitution, omission, or addition evidenced in the words. Then I give you the IPA version
of the pronunciation variation and then finally the IPA version if pronounced correctly. By "correctly," I mean the pronunciation preferred by most people in the United States.

There are bound to be places where you disagree with the
way I have chosen to list a word as correct because of the way

folks in your area pronounce the word. That's OK. Please make a note of it and send it to me. I will be glad to include it in the next edition.

**Figure 9.1**

# Words with Pronunciation Variations

|  |  | The variation | More appropriate |
|---|---|---|---|
| absorb | /z/ used for /s/ | [ 'æb 'zɔrb ] | [ æb 'sɔrb ] |
| absurd | /z/ used for /s/ | [ 'æb 'zɝd ] | [ æb 'sɝd ] |
| abyss | /æ/ used for /ə/ | [ 'æ bəs ] | [ ə 'bɪs ] |
| accuracy | /j/ omitted | [ 'æk ɚ si] | [ 'æk 'jɚ ə 'si ] |
| actually | /ʃ/ used for /tʃ/ | [ 'æk ʃɚ lə ] | [ 'æk tʃə lə ] |
| adversary | /a/ used for /ɚ/ | [ 'æd və sɛr ə ] | [ 'æd vɚ sɛr ə ] |
| aesthetic | /t/ used for /θ/ | [ 'æs 'tɛt ək ] | [ æs 'θɛt ək ] |
| alone | /e/ used for /ə/ | [ 'e 'lon ] | [ ə 'lon ] |
| almost | /l/ omitted | [ 'ɒ 'most ] | [ 'ɒl 'most ] |
| always | /l/ omitted | [ 'ɒ 'wez ] | [ 'ɒl 'wez ] |
| amnesia | /z/ used for /s/ | [ æm 'niz jə ] | [ 'æm 'niʒ jə ] |
| archipelago | /tʃ/ used for /k/ | [ artʃ ə 'pɛl ə go ] | [ 'ark ə 'pɛl ə go ] |
| ask | /k/ omitted | [ 'æs ] | [ 'æsk ] |
| bag | /ɛ/ used for /æ/ | [ 'bɛg ] | [ 'bæg ] |
| baptize | /b/ used for /p/ | [ 'bæb 'taɪz ] | [ 'bæp 'taɪz ] |
| beautiful | /i/ used for /ə/ | [ 'bju 'ti fəl ] | [ 'bju tə fəl ] |
| beautiful | /i/ added | [ 'bi 'ju tə fəl ] | [ 'bju tə fəl ] |
| beige | /dʒ/ used for /ʒ/ | [ 'bedʒ ] | [ 'beʒ ] |
| bird | /ɜ/ used for /ɝ/ | [ 'bɜd ] | [ 'bɝd ] |
| birds | /ts/ used for /dz/ | [ 'bɝts ] | [ 'bɝdz ] |
| birthday | /f/used for /θ/ | [ 'bɝf 'de ] | [ 'bɝθ 'de ] |
| breakfast | /k/ omitted | [ 'brɛ fəst ] | [ 'brɛk fəst ] |
| bridges | /s/ used for /z/ | [ 'brɪ dʒəs ] | [ 'brɪ dʒəz ] |
| brochure | /ɚ/ used for /ur/ | [ 'bro ʃɚ ] | [ bro 'ʃjur ] |
| camouflage | /dʒ/ used for /ʒ/ | [ 'kæm ə 'fladʒ ] | [ 'kæm ə 'flaʒ ] |
| candidate | /d/ omitted | [ 'kæn ə 'det ] | [ 'kæn də 'det ] |
| can't | /e/ used for /æ/ | [ 'kent ] | [ 'kænt ] |
| cashmere | /ʒ/ used for /ʃ/ | [ 'kæʒ 'mɪr ] | [ 'kæʃ mɪr ] |
| cavalry | /l/ omitted | [ 'kæv ə ri ] | [ 'kæ vəl 'ri ] |
| center | /t/ omitted | [ 'sɛn ɚ ] | [ 'sɛn tɚ ] |

| center | /ɪ/ used for /ɛ/ | [ 'sɪn tɚ ] | [ 'sɛn tɚ ] |
|---|---|---|---|
| chagrin | /tʃ/ used for /ʃ/ | [ tʃə 'grɪn ] | [ ʃə 'grɪn ] |
| chasm | /tʃ/ used for /k/ | [ 'tʃæz əm ] | [ 'kæz əm ] |
| chimney | /l/ used for /n/ | [ 'tʃɪm li ] | [ 'tʃɪm ni ] |
| corsage | /dʒ/ used for /ʒ/ | [ 'kɔr 'sadʒ ] | [ 'kɔr 'saʒ ] |
| couldn't | /t/ used for /d/ | [ 'kʊt ənt ] | [ 'kʊd ənt ] |
| cuisine | /w/ omitted | [ 'ku 'zin ] | [ 'kwɪ 'zin ] |
| darn | /–/ used for /r/ | [ 'dɑn ] | [ 'dɑrn ] |
| dawn | /aw/ used for /ɒ/ | [ 'daw ən ] | [ 'dɒn ] |
| depths | /θ/ omitted | [ 'dɛps ] | [ 'dɛpθs ] |
| diphtheria | /p/ used for /f/ | [ 'dɪp 'θɪr i ə ] | [ 'dɪf 'θɪr i ə ] |
| diphthong | /p/ used for /f/ | [ 'dɪp 'θɒŋ ] | [ 'dɪf 'θɒŋ ] |
| docile | /aɪə/ used for /ə/ | [ 'dɑ 'saɪ əl ] | [ 'dɑ səl ] |
| drama | /æ/ used for /ɑ/ | [ 'dræmə ] | [ 'drɑmə ] |
| egg | /e/ used for /ɛ/ | [ 'eg ] | [ 'ɛg ] |
| enough | /i/ used for /ə/ | [ 'i 'nʌf ] | [ ə 'nʌf ] |
| environment | /n/ omitted | [ 'ɛn 'vaɪr 'mənt ] | [ 'ɛn 'vaɪ rən 'mənt ] |
| error | /ɚ/ omitted | [ 'ɛr ] | [ 'ɛrɚ ] |
| et cetera | /k/ used for /t/ | [ 'ɛk 'sɛt ə rə ] | [ 'ɛt 'sɛt ə rə ] |
| familiar | /l/ omitted | [ fə'mɪ jɚ ] | [ fə 'mɪl jɚ ] |
| figure | /j/ omitted | [ 'fɪg ɚ ] | [ 'fɪg jɚ ] |
| fill | /ɛ/ used for /ɪ/ | [ 'fɛl ] | [ 'fɪl ] |
| finale | /æ/ used for /ɑ/ | [ fɪn 'ælə ] | [ fə 'nɑlə ] |
| finger | /g/ omitted | [ 'fɪŋ ɚ ] | [ 'fɪŋ gɚ ] |
| fruit | /u/ used for /u/ | [ 'frut ] | [ 'frut ] |
| gesturing | /g/ used for /dʒ/ | [ 'ges tʃɚ ɪŋ ] | [ 'dʒes tʃɚ ɪŋ ] |
| get | /ɪ/ used for /ɛ/ | [ 'gɪt ] | [ 'gɛt ] |
| goblet | /ə/ added | [ 'gɑb ə 'let ] | [ 'gɑb 'lət ] |
| government | /n/ omitted | [ 'gʌv ɚ mənt] | [ 'gʌv ən mənt ] |
| grasped | /p/ omitted | [ 'græst ] | [ 'græspt ] |
| guarantee | /ɛ/ used for /æ/ | [ 'ger ən 'ti ] | [ gærən 'ti ] |
| heat | /ɪ/ used for /i/ | [ 'hɪt ] | [ 'hit ] |
| Heather | /f/ used for /ð/ | [ 'hɛ fɚ ] | [ 'hɛ ðɚ ] |
| height | /θ/ used for /t/ | [ 'haɪθ] | [ 'haɪt ] |
| humane | /h/ omitted | [ 'ju men ] | [ 'hju men ] |
| immobile | /aɪ/ used for /ə/ | [ 'ɪ 'mo 'baɪ əl ] | [ ɪ 'mo bəl ] |
| important | /r/ omitted | [ 'ɪm 'po tənt ] | [ 'ɪm 'pɔr tənt ] |
| impotent | /o/ used for /ə/ | [ 'ɪm 'po tənt ] | [ 'ɪm pə tənt ] |
| interesting | /t/ omitted | [ 'ɪn ə rɛst əŋ ] | [ 'ɪn tɚ 'rɛst əŋ ] |
| jaw | /ɑ/ used for /ɒ/ | [ 'dʒɑ ] | [ 'dʒɒ ] |
| kindergarten | /d/ omitted | [ 'kɪn ɚ gɑr tən ] | [ 'kɪn dɚ 'gɑr tən] |

| larynx | /nɪ/ used for /ɪŋ/ | [ 'lɛr 'nɪks ] | [ 'lɛr 'ɪŋks ] |
|---|---|---|---|
| least | /ɪ/ used for /i/ | [ 'lɪst ] | [ 'list ] |
| leave | /f/ used for /v/ | [ 'lif ] | [ 'liv ] |
| lecithin | /kt/ used for /s/ | [ 'lɛk tə sən ] | [ 'lɛs ə θən ] |
| length | /nθ/ used for /ŋk/ | [ 'lɛnθ ] | [ 'lɛŋkθ ] |
| liaison | /ə/ used for /e/ | [ 'li ə 'zɒn] | [ 'li 'e 'zɒn ] |
| liberate | /v/ used for /b/ | [ 'lɪv ɚ 'ret ] | [ 'lɪb ɚ 'ret ] |
| library | /r/ omitted | [ 'laɪ 'bɛr ə ] | [ 'laɪ 'brɛr ə ] |
| little | /w/ used for /l/ | [ 'wɪt əl ] | [ 'lɪt əl ] |
| many | /ɪ/ used for /ɛ/ | [ 'mɪn ə ] | [ 'mɛn ə ] |
| meadow | /ə/ used for /o/ | [ 'mɛ də ] | [ 'mɛ do ] |
| measure | /e/ used for /ɛ/ | [ 'mɛʒ ɚ ] | [ 'mɛʒ ɚ ] |
| mens | /s/ used for /z/ | [ 'mɪns ] | [ 'mɛnz ] |
| mischievous | /i/ used for /ə/ | [ 'mɪs 'tʃi və əs ] | [ 'mɪs tʃɪ vəs ] |
| miserable | /r/ used for /ɚ/ | [ 'mɪs rə bəl ] | [ 'mɪz ɚ ə bəl ] |
| missile | /aɪ/ used for /ə/ | [ 'mɪs aɪəl ] | [ 'mɪs əl ] |
| months | /θ/ omitted | [ 'mʌns] | [ 'mʌnθs ] |
| nuclear | /ə/ added | [ 'nuk ə lɚ ] | [ 'nuk 'liɚ ] |
| of | /f/ used for /v/ | [ 'ʌf ] | [ 'ʌv ] |
| over | /ə/ used for /ɚ/ | [ 'ovə ] | [ 'ovɚ ] |
| pillow | /ə/ used for /o/ | [ 'pɪlə ] | [ 'pɪlo ] |
| pretend | /ɚ/ used for /r / | [ 'pɚ tend ] | [ 'prə tend ] |
| probably | /b/ omitted | [ 'prɑb lə ] | [ 'prɑb əb lə ] |
| poem | /ɪ/ omitted | [ 'pom ] | [ 'po ɪm ] |
| psalm | /l/ added | [ 'sɑlm ] | [ 'sɑm ] |
| pumpkin | /n/ used for /m/ | [ 'pʌn kən ] | [ pʌmp kən ] |
| quarter | /d/ used for /t/ | [ 'kwɔr dɚ ] | [ 'kwɔr tɚ ] |
| recognize | /g/ omitted | [ 'rɛk ə 'naɪz ] | [ 'rɛk əg 'naɪz ] |
| register | /d/ used for /ʤ/ | [ 'rɛd ə stɚ ] | [ 'rɛʤ əs tɚ ] |
| rural | /w/ used for /r/ | [ 'wɝ·əl ] | [ 'rɝ· əl ] |
| sandwich | /m/ used for /nd/ | [ 'sæm 'wɪtʃ ] | [ 'sænd 'wɪtʃ ] |
| secretary | /r/ omitted | [ 'sɛkə 'tɛr ə ] | [ 'sɛk rə tɛr ə ] |
| sentence | /t/ omitted | [ 'sɛn əns ] | [ 'sɛn təns ] |
| someone | /w/ omitted | [ 'sʌm ən ] | [ 'sʌm 'wən ] |
| statistics | /s/ added | [ stə 'stɪ stəks ] | [ stə 'tɪst əks ] |
| stream | /ʃ/ used for /s/ | [ 'ʃtrim ] | [ 'strim ] |
| street | /k/ used for /t/ | [ 'skrit ] | [ 'strit ] |
| strength | /n/ used for /ŋ/ | [ 'strɛnθ ] | [ 'strɪŋkθ ] |
| suggest | /g/ omitted | [ sə 'ʤest ] | [ 'sʌg 'ʤest ] |
| tail | /ɛ/ used for /e/ | [ 'tɛl ] | [ 'te əl ] |
| tapestry | /e/ used for /æ/ | [ 'tep əs 'tri ] | [ 'tæp əs 'tri ] |

| | | | |
|---|---|---|---|
| tests | omitted /t/ | [ 'tes ] | [ 'tes̱ts ] |
| tests | /ə/ added | [ 'testəs ] | [ 'tests ] |
| that | /d/ used for /ð/ | [ 'dæt ] | [ 'ðæt] |
| then | /θ/ used for /ð/ | [ 'θen ] | [ 'ðen ] |
| then | /ə/ added | [ 'ðɛ ən ] | [ 'ðen ] |
| thin | /ð/ used for /θ/ | [ 'ðɪn ] | [ 'θɪn ] |
| tool | /ʌ/ used for /u/ | [ 'tʌl ] | [ 'tu̱ əl ] |
| wash | /ɔr/ used for /ɑ/ | [ 'wɔrʃ ] | [ 'wɒʃ ] |
| watt | /ʍ/ used for /w/ | [ 'ʍat ] | [ 'wat ] |
| wedding | /n/ used for /ŋ/ | [ 'wɛd ən ] | [ 'wɛd ɪŋ ] |
| window | /ə/ used for /o/ | [ 'wɪn də ] | [ 'wɪn do̱ ] |
| what | /w/ used for /ʍ/ | [ 'wat ] | [ 'ʍat ] |
| when | /ʍɪ/ used for /ʍɛ/ | [ 'wɪn ] | [ 'ʍen ] |
| word | /ʌ/ used for /ɝ/ | [ 'wʌd ] | [ 'wɝ̱d ] |
| writhe | /v/ used for /ð/ | [ 'raɪv ] | [ 'raɪð̱ ] |
| youngish | /g/ added | [ 'jʌŋ gəʃ ] | [ 'jʌŋ ɪʃ ] |

# 10 THE SPEAKER'S BODY

## DRESS: LOOKING GOOD!

The most immediate part of the first impression an audience will have of you is what you are wearing. If your attire meets the expectations of the audience, it will be more accepting of your message. It will then seek other information variables as it evaluates you as a speaker. If your attire significantly deviates from audience members' expectations and they can't justify the exception, your attempt at successful communication may be over. This is true for most American audiences. They simply are less likely to attend to your message.

Whether we like it or not, audiences will critique us, to some extent, on what we are wearing. With that in mind, let's go through some basic ideas for appropriate dress on the platform:

1. Dress at least as formally as or slightly more formally than the speaking situation calls for. That way, you'll always meet audience expectations.
2. Dress comfortably (and this includes shoes!). Make sure that what you are wearing fits and doesn't need constant attention or adjustment while you are speaking. This includes ties, belts, zippers, straps, and jewelry. Remember, if you are adjusting items of clothing while speaking, the audience focus will be on this movement. Comfort-

able clothing, including shoes, will allow your movement on stage to appear natural. If I doesn't fit, don't wear it.

3. Don't forget that your dress is part of your visual aid. What you have on should complement your message, not overpower it or underrate it. If your attire calls attention to itself and that is not your intent, your audience members will not be focusing on your message.

4. Always dress in good taste to make a good impression on your audience. This may call for attention to length of hemlines or trousers, tightness of clothing, appropriate necklines, the length of your tie, and the cleanliness of what you wear and yourself (make sure your clothes are pressed or ironed and make sure you are clean shaven or neatly trimmed). Be aware of your fashion combinations. Do your pants and sport coat match? Do you have a pleasing combination of stripes, patterns, and colors?

5. Dress for a speaking engagement with temperature in mind. Remember that there will be stage lights or heat from overhead projectors that will keep you warm. What you wear should not make you perspire heavily on stage.

6. How you are dressed will also have an impact on you. Are you comfortable? Are your pants too tight? Are they too loose? Are they zipped? Is your jacket too heavy? Are you wearing too many layers? What does your clothing do to the way you feel and behave?

So, you are what you wear? Maybe. Maybe not. But what you choose to wear does become a part of what your audience perceives as you. There are several "dress for success" books and magazine articles available. Study them if you need that kind of information. Folks who will be part of your audience are also a good source of information regarding the appropriateness of what you have chosen to wear for that particular occasion. Most clothing stores have salespeople who will eagerly check out your clothing choice combinations. This is especially true if you purchase items from them.

## MOVEMENT THAT COMMUNICATES

For most people, if it's moving, we will watch it. If you want to steal the show or upstage someone, all you have to do is move. The polite standard calls for everyone but the one speaking to be quiet and not to move. But those who want the attention know that sometimes physical movement can attract more attention than words.

This is valuable information for a speaker. A speaker's movement can take attention away from the content of the message. The speaker's movements and words should be consistent. The movement should support or reinforce the words of the message. Let's take a look at some instances in which movements might overpower the words spoken:

1. Backing up while making a point may cause you to lose emphasis in your message. Step forward to connect with your audience. Be careful not to jut your head forward to convey interest; this works against keeping good posture. You can convey interest while still using good posture; use subtle movements to do this. It is best to bend slightly from the waist rather that rolling forward at your shoulders.

2. Pacing back and forth when the movement is unrelated to the content can be a distracting element in your delivery. A speaker should move with a purpose, not just to be moving. Move to reinforce the verbal message.

3. Stiff mechanical movements that don't match the rhythm pattern of the message can be distracting and may also appear awkward and take away from any "natural" appearance you would like to give your audience.

4. Remaining "statue-still" while sharing activities and/or emotions may cause you to appear uninterested or detached from the members of the audience.

5. Moving toward an audience helps a speaker to establish, maintain, and strengthen identification with that audi-

ence. Even if the physical arrangement is such that the speaker is unable to be within close proximity to the audience, the appearance of the speaker trying to get closer to the audience will help with identification. Moving to the side or in front of the lectern or stepping forward to the edge of the stage can make a big difference.

6.  In the event that you are seated while speaking, leaning forward in your chair will help. Moving back in your chair, even a little, diminishes the feeling of identification. Sitting back in your chair slows the identification down and crossing your legs as you do so kills it.

7.  Be aware of your position in relation to your audience. Sometimes your stage is elevated and you are physically above your audience. Although you may be unable to change this setting, don't compound the problem by holding your head too erect so that you are literally looking down your nose at the audience.

8.  Avoid tugging, pulling, and adjusting clothing. We will say it again, "If it doesn't fit, don't wear it." These movements may appear minor, but they are very noticeable and they very easily distract your listeners' attention from your message. Remember, "If it's moving, people will watch it."

9.  This may seem comical or even disgusting, but I have seen this done in a not-so-becoming fashion. Be aware of scratching body parts! Here's a little-known fact regarding the act of scratching: you can scratch anywhere on your body as long as you don't look at your fingers when you finish! The act of scratching may make your audience members uncomfortable, but looking at your fingers after the act will repulse them. Test the reliability of this phenomenon. When you are with a small group of acquaintances or perhaps with strangers, try it out. This calls for a little hamming it up and cutting loose, so have fun! With facial grimaces, pretend to dig deeply into your ear with your little finger, and then return your hand to your side. Wait a few seconds, then glance quickly at your little finger. Most onlookers will moan and be visibly disgusted. This should be a strong reminder not to do similar body scratching on the platform.

Movement is an often neglected component in delivery. Movement should be perceived as natural and spontaneous. Using movement that is comfortable to the speaker yet pleasing to an audience takes time, practice, and thought. Always keep in mind that distance from and above your audience are important variables. Be sure to use them to your advantage.

## GESTURES: TO SUPPORT THE POINTS YOU ARE MAKING

Gestures should be consistent and congruent with the meaning of the words being shared. Audiences tend to divert their attention to watch things that are moving or easily noticeable. You want the audience to focus on your face and the words you are sharing. If your hand is making random movements that lack purpose or emphasis, the audience will watch your inconsistent movement and miss the content.

When you are first practicing and rehearsing your speech, remember that your use or lack of use of gestures is also being rehearsed. So while you are going over your notes, or even practicing a manuscript, when you feel gestures with your hands or your face are needed to illustrate a point, just do it! The rehearsal will reinforce those gestures for later use when you actually deliver your speech. Waiting to include gestures until your final rehearsal or the actual performance itself will generally result in artificial-looking movements. You must focus on the content of your message while you are delivering your speech. You won't have time to think about or make decisions about gestures during the real thing. So, you will more than likely feel uncomfortable as you deliver these gestures without plenty of rehearsal.

During your initial practice sessions, monitor the size and placement of those gestures that add to the meaning of your message. You want rather large definite movements for each gesture. The bigger the audience, the bigger the gestures should be. If you are using your index finger with your palm held toward your audience to indicate the first point of your presentation, make sure you raise your forearm slightly up and away from your body. Continue to use your hand gestures to provide visual signposts as you progress through the other points of your speech.

However, there are some gestures you need to avoid using excessively. The small "palm-up-rolling-the-thumb-to-the-side" gesture is a movement you need to pay special attention not to overuse. When doing this gesture, the speaker's arm is held out in front of the body and the majority of movement is in the wrist to turn the hand out to the side. It looks as if you are fanning smoke or an odor. If it is repeated too often it looks like the fin of a fish and can be very distracting to your audience. Continuing to point in random directions or to the audience for each point made can also be very distracting. Clicking a ball-point pen, tapping a ring on the lectern, jingling keys or change in your pockets, and crossing your arms are to be avoided unless they emphasize a point you are making.

To be effective, most gestures should be made above your elbow and out away from your body. The ideal position for most gestures is within a forearm's length away from your body. For variety, on occasion use your full arm length and contrast that with a few gestures next to your body. Variety in gestures keeps audiences interested. When you don't use variety, audience members can easily become caught up in predicting your next gesture or body movement. This, of course, means they are not focusing on the content of your message.

Facial gestures are mandatory to reinforce, amplify, and call attention to points you think are important in your message. The first consideration has to be awareness of your general countenance. This will require you to take a serious look at yourself in the mirror and to ask yourself some questions.

And be honest! Does your face, in its relaxed condition, look happy or sad? Most of us have never asked the question. Take the opportunity to check the perception of others as they reflect on the condition of your habitual facial gestures.

Many people seem always to look happy; it's almost like they have a permanent smile on their faces. Their countenances are generally perceived by others as bright and happy. Then, there are the rest of us. The corners of our mouths just naturally drop or we have large pouch-like cheeks. This is not bad; it just means we need to be aware of this and make some minor changes when we speak. We may need to make deliberate efforts to smile more or not to squint our eyes when we are on stage.

We must also take into account our facial gestures when we speak. If our faces are inanimate, we may be perceived as being angry or grumbling when we talk. Some of us tend to articulate sounds in the backs of our mouths, so we don't move our lips very much when we speak. Our faces are basically immobile. If our faces aren't moved, there is a good chance our audiences won't be either.

Regardless of what you do to enhance the appearance of your face, the best advice I can give is to encourage you to smile a lot and smile often. In addition to making you look better, it will actually make you feel better. Smiling will catch people's attention. Smiling is also one of the triggers that releases healing endorphins in your body.

OK, for those really hard-core folks out there, this is for you. You don't carry a happy-looking face. You aren't a smiler either. What can you do? To soften the harsh look of your face, tighten the cheek muscles at the corners of your mouth. Check yourself in a mirror. You aren't trying to give yourself a smile; just level the corners of your mouth so you don't look like you are going to bite or be sick. If you have ever had anyone ask you if you were feeling OK, they may be responding to the "sick" look on your face.

## EYE CONTACT: DO I HAVE TO LOOK AT THEM?

How many times as children and adults have we heard someone say to us, "Just look 'em straight in the eyes and tell 'em how you feel"? We've used that advice when we've had to tell someone the truth about something or when we just felt it was time to get something off our chests. Regardless of the situation, most people feel that if someone is able to look them in the eyes, that person is telling the truth. Most people believe that they can judge a person's character and intentions based on this simple act. And so the same holds true for speakers. You've got to "look 'em straight in the eyes and tell 'em how you feel" if you want to be perceived as credible!

Many people may react to this piece of advice by saying, "Easier said than done." For some speakers, this can be difficult. Some people just have a natural tendency to look away when they are talking to someone. And some of those people have grown up to be professional speakers. While on the platform, not looking your audience members in the eyes can be troublesome for those audience members who have to make decisions about your credibility. If your eye contact is shifty, are you shifty too? We may be looking up, down, right, or left as we recall what we are going to say next. If that is a consistent pattern for you, it is necessary for you to adjust your head position so that you don't look like you are avoiding the audience.

The advice for eye contact is very basic and straightforward: Look in the eyes of your audience members. You can't identify with members of your audience unless you make eye contact with them. Don't allow yourself to habitually look at their foreheads, at their chins, or over their heads at the back wall. Where you are visually focusing is where your audience will focus. When your audience members are turning around in their chairs to see who is in the back of the room, this may be a good indication of the focus you have created in your presentation. The good news is that they are focused on what you are focused on (the back wall). The bad news is that unless you look at them they will continue to focus back there and not attend to your message.

Make sure you consider the size of your audience. If your audience is small, the task of making eye contact is made simpler for you. You will be able to make eye contact with all the members of your audience. If your audience is very large, your job is a bit more difficult. It is not necessary to make eye contact with every person in the room, but you do need to make eye contact with each section in the room. Don't just stare at one or two people throughout your entire presentation. You may make them feel uncomfortable and the other audience members will begin looking at them instead of you. Don't forget about your folks in the corner, the ones in the back, the one or two people partially hidden behind the projection screen, or the lady in the big hat. Keep in mind that these folks may have selected these seats on purpose; they may want to listen but not want to be involved. These are the people you will need to make a conscious effort to make eye contact with in an effort to gain their attention and interest. (But, of course, don't neglect the others in the room.)

If you are reading your script or spending a lot of time focusing on your notes, you will be denying your audience the opportunity to identify with you. Those quick glances up and out at the audience really can't be considered eye contact. You are looking, but the glance is so quick, you aren't seeing anything. Those glances may be polite, but the distance they help establish between you and your audience is generally not to your advantage.

The frequency of your eye blinking and the duration of the blink can keep the attention of your audience on your eye movement behavior rather than on the content of your message. If your blinks are too frequent, you could be perceived as unsure of yourself, having to think too hard, having something in your eye, being flirty, or not having a brain in your head. If you hold the duration of a blink too long (keeping your eyes closed), the audience might perceive you as thinking about what to say, being tired, being not "with the program," or avoiding audience contact.

As speakers, we are passionate about our topics. We deeply desire our audiences to be equally as excited as we are. Our intensity might show as we open our eyes really wide and a lot of the whites of our eyes show to the audience. Audiences perceive that behavior as being scared stiff, being "crazy as a loon," staring really hard, reciting from memory, or daydreaming.

Probably the best way to check or monitor your eye contact is to use a video camera. As you view the videotape, turn down the volume and do frequency counts of the most prevalent eye movement behaviors. A blink every 5 to 10 seconds will keep your eyes moist and not call attention to itself. When you don't blink often enough, some may perceive you as staring or daydreaming. Even though you may feel you don't need to blink for your physical comfort, you might consider doing so to keep from distancing your audience. Be sure to look for too many blinks—remember that too many blinks could be perceived as distracting.

# EXTERNAL FACTORS

The speaker's primary task is to encourage audience members to create in their minds the same mental image the speaker wants to share. As a speaker, it is your first challenge to structure your message clearly and to choose words, sentences, and paragraphs that will help make that image clear. Then you have to consider how those words are said: voice qualities, rate, pitch, volume, and pronunciation. Beyond these considerations, you must question how your appearance will help the audience to create the appropriate mental images.

Let's assume that you have presented yourself to an audience and that it is accepting of you and your desire to share your message. It is not distracted by you or your appearance. What else is to be done to help the audience members "see" your message?

You must now consider the external factors—the factors outside yourself—that will add to the audience members' image of you and the mental images you want them to create. You should take into account the physical makeup of the room and its arrangement, visual aids that you bring to the presentation, and the sound amplification facilities. All these factors can work together to help or hurt the images your message conveys.

## ROOM SETTING: YOU WANT
## THE AUDIENCE TO BE WHERE?

What are the best room arrangements and how can a speaker use particular room setups to his or her advantage? Most table and chair arrangements are dictated by the size of the audience and the unique properties of the room. However, the ideal arrangement is to have the speaker as close to the audience as possible and as high up as practical. There can be a few exceptions to these rules, so we'll take a look at different arrangements and how they can affect a speaker's presentation.

What are some limitations or problems a speaker may encounter when addressing the idea of room arrangements? If the room is a long, narrow basement chamber with support columns every 10 feet in all directions, that is a given limitation. If the chairs are bolted to the floor, the seating arrangement won't be an issue. At other times, changing the arrangement of the room may not be an option for the speaker due to time constraints and other restrictions. So it may be necessary for a speaker to discuss such concerns with the meeting planner beforehand. Having thought through the audience arrangement you prefer can help your meeting planner set things up for you. If you have warned him or her in advance, making changes once you get there will be acceptable. If how your audience is seated does not matter to you, you will have to be accepting of the room arrangement as it is.

When considering the size of the audience, what is the best arrangement for tables and chairs? If your audience is a large one, particular details of arranging the tables and/or chairs is not necessary. For such large numbers, it is very difficult to be creative with seating arrangements. The most important thing to do is to get them as close to the speaker as possible without violating the personal space of the closest audience members. It is best to stay back about three feet from the front audience members but still address your remarks to the entire group.

If the audience is going to be smaller than 50 people and it is possible to move chairs and tables around, do so. Whatever table and chair layout you choose, make sure that your audience members all have a good, clear sight line in your direction. You may want to set up an aisle down the middle and angle the tables. This is effective if you are planning to move closer to the audience members in the back but you don't want your front-row people to have to turn around to see you. Regular theatre seating, with your audience lined up parallel to the stage area with no center aisle, works great if you are sure you will be moving back and forth on the stage to encourage participation.

As the number of audience members decreases, your decisions about the room arrangement will become easier. If the group is in the 25-or-so size range, you have many more options on chair arrangement, assuming the room will allow. A semicircle works very well if you really desire participation out of each member of your audience.

If the number in your audience is small, the question of getting you as high as possible isn't an issue. Most people will be able to see you without any obstructions, so it won't be necessary for you to be elevated above them. If the audience is in a semicircle and all members can see you, even sitting down is possible and acceptable. Be aware that sitting down, especially for short presentations, reduces the credibility of the speaker. But if you are doing a half-day or full-day seminar and you are doing most of the talking, the change in body position will probably be welcomed by you and the audience. Be sure that the audience can see you if you do decide to sit down—and don't forget to use good posture— don't slouch or lean back; this will cause you to appear inattentive and fatigued.

As the audience number grows, the opportunity to see you clearly will diminish. Then it will be necessary to seek some form of elevation so that the audience's sight lines can be available to you. I am always disappointed when I am in an audience of over 100 people and the speaker chooses to step down off the platform in front of the first row to explain a specific point. The physical position of the speaker denies the majority of the audience an opportunity to see him or her and causes the audience not to feel included. Those who can't see the speaker feel cheated. Some will feel even less than worthy; everyone wants to feel attended to equally.

## VISUAL AIDS: MY AUDIENCE HAS GOT TO SEE THIS

You are the message that the audience must first react to and digest. Even if you are "walking your talk" and you haven't distracted the audience, their minds may still wander. The audience is free to listen to you at this point. However, illustrating your message visually will allow your audience to explore with you this mental image you are trying to share. Visual aids help hold the attention of the audience. They also add interest, clarity, and credibility to your message. Visual aids can help your audiences remember the important points of your message.

In addition to amplifying the message, visuals aids assist the speaker, too. They often give the speaker more confidence. Visual aids may contain lists or main points that can serve as a subtle note set. But they can also temporarily divert the attention of the audience from the speaker to the information contained on them for a short time. This "break" can give the speaker an opportunity to reorganize his or her thoughts and prepare himself or herself for the next major point.

Poster boards, flip charts, overheads, hand-outs, and chalkboards are by far the most popular visual aids used by speakers. They are easy to prepare, easy to use, and quickly received by audiences. As a speaker, your goal is to stay in control of your visuals so that fewer things are able to go wrong. Just be sure you have practiced your presentation using the visual aids. Keep your focus on the audience and let your visual aid support your words. Don't keep looking at it so that it becomes the focus.

If you have the equipment available and the expertise necessary, make use of technological possibilities. Computers and their accompanying programs are spectacular if they are suited to your purposes. Programs that allow you to create graphs, tables, artwork, and even entire visual presentations are most helpful. But make sure your equipment is in good working order and is up and running. Technical difficulties can sometimes turn an attempt at very professional visual aids into a nightmare. If you know how to use the equipment and can troubleshoot potential problems, let your creativity run wild!

Video and audio clips can help an audience experience the sights and sounds of your message even better than just talking about them can. Again, be familiar with the equipment and its use. Murphy's Law is always in effect! If anything can go wrong, it probably will. With computer screens and projection facilities, even the best of visual images can be difficult to see if light conditions in the room are not appropriate. Even simple slide projectors with front or rear projection need to be checked carefully because of the possibility of too much light on the screen.

Often, the best visual aid is the object itself. If this is a possibility, make sure that the object isn't too heavy or too bulky since this will cause you difficulties if you are required to maneuver it on stage. Also, see to it that the object doesn't upstage you. A visual aid having moving parts, making noise, or containing many parts or details will distract your audience's attention for longer periods of time than necessary.

Regardless of the visual elements you have chosen to use in your presentations, make sure they do indeed amplify the intended message. The object, the print, or the picture must be big enough to be seen clearly from the back row. This requires the visual aids to be uncluttered, with only one thought or point per visual. Be careful of long elaborate lists. The visuals must look sharp and clear, have an air of quality, and be in good taste. Keep them simple and appropriate. Don't use a variety of type fonts or too many different colors on a single visual.

Remember, you are the speaker. The visuals amplify the meaning you are trying to share; it's not you trying to amplify the visual aids.

## THE PUBLIC ADDRESS SYSTEM: BUT CAN THEY UNDERSTAND ME?

Sound systems are a great innovation and help by making sound available to larger areas and larger numbers of people. Once again, it is important to remember that they are electrical and mechanical and that problems do exist. If you aren't a master at operating or troubleshooting the sound equipment, make sure you have someone available who is.

You should also give consideration to how you use microphones. Don't be a slave to a microphone mounted on the podium. Don't allow your head to jut forward in order to position yourself near it. This awkward body positioning will affect the sound of your voice. Instead, position the microphone so that it will pick up your sound when your body is positioned most efficiently with good posture. When you allow the microphone to readjust your body positioning and to take your focus away from the presentation, the microphone can become the center of the audience's attention. The microphone should be an unobtrusive portion of the equipment available. Don't let it be the focus of attention!

# 12 STAY HEALTHY
## It Is Your Choice

For right now, let's take some time to discuss ways that we can take care of ourselves and be healthy. We're going to look at ways you can be good to your body. Taking care of ourself does require work and commitment. To some people, this can be a daunting task. So this discussion is also about some other choices and NOT just about changing vocal or movement behaviors. As a professional speaker making changes in some of those other behaviors (such as not smoking), nutrition/diet (avoiding certain foods before speaking), exercise (not just doing aerobic exercise but exercises for posture, pitch, breathing, etc.) could save our lives. Ultimately, we've got to **look like we are walking our talk**. But let's look at a few simple things we can do to take care of our bodies. When we take care of our bodies (and that includes our voices), the results are numerous and our speaking careers and our spirits will be rewarded.

### WALK YOUR TALK: THEY WILL BELIEVE IT WHEN THEY SEE IT

Throughout this book, we've talked about different exercises we can do to help strengthen and improve the condition of our voices and our bodies. Right now, let's sit up (not slouched down like a couch potato) and relax, give some much needed attention to ourselves, and talk about things we

can do for our bodies and our minds. These tips and suggestions are little ideas I've acquired and used through the years.
Some of these strategies may work for you better than others.
You may have your own health regimens that you follow to
keep your bodies and voices in shape. Whether you have
your own set of guidelines for healthy living or you're trying
to develop a lifestyle for healthy living, let's think about
those ways that we can treat ourselves better and take care of
our bodies.

For a large part of our lives, many of us have heard that
we should eat right. But what exactly does this mean? We all
know the foods that are good for us, such as pastas, baked
foods (as opposed to being fried or baked goods), fruits, and
vegetables. And probably more than we'd like to admit, we
are very familiar with those foods that aren't good for us.
Knowing what is good and bad for us to eat is usually not the
problem. The problem is being in control of the decision
process regarding what we eat.

Many of us eat for the wrong reasons: "I think it's time to
eat." "I'm not hungry now but I won't have time to eat later."
"I'm nervous." "I'm excited." "I'm scared." "I'm bored." The
wrong-reasons-to-eat list is long. For whatever reason, we
convince ourselves that we have to eat NOW. Obviously, we
can say that our eating patterns are heavily determined by
forces outside ourselves. Our emotional state dictates what
and how much we eat. The most difficult task is controlling
what we eat instead of being controlled by eating.

As we listen to our bodies and pay attention to them, we
begin to recognize our bodies' limits. We begin to recognize
our bodies' patterns and tendencies also. Some people eat
when they don't feel there is anything to do. To combat this
problem, make a list of your favorite activities. Your list might
contain walking the dog, working in the garden, playing on
the computer, or doing some kind of needlework. Place this

list on your refrigerator so that it can be seen when you go hunting for "just a little snack." This will help you to recognize when you're eating out of boredom and it will encourage you to engage in one of these activities. If your favorite activity is passively watching TV, there's not too much advice anyone can give you. You just have to get yourself up and off the couch!

We all have these little ideas or tricks that help keep ourselves in line. My solution to snacking is to be active. Look for other things to do than food. Others may choose to keep a journal to probe what is really going on in their minds. Document what you eat, when you were hungry, when you ate, and what mood you were in as you identified your hunger just before you ate. This allows you to take stock of what you eat and to look for certain eating patterns. Do I eat when I'm nervous? Do I snack mainly at night? Whatever your little trick is to control your eating, make sure it's a friendly one. Don't allow it to bring you down or make you miserable. Keep it positive!

Some quick reminders for you to consider if you know you eat more than you should. Understand your body well enough to know when you are hungry. Not head hunger but real body hunger. Take the time to feel it. Know when you are full. THEN stop eating. Period. Eat only when you are hungry, and then stop eating.

For those times when hunger does strike and a snack is necessary, always keep a supply of healthy, filling snacks around. One of my favorite snacks is gorp. What is gorp? You make it by combining three or four different cereals. You can add raisins, too, to give it a sweet taste. Avoid adding the M&M's®. Be sure the cereals you use don't contain too much sugar. Some gorp recipes suggest adding nuts, but beware, they are very high in fat. I try to keep low-fat, fruit-filled snack bars in the car and in my brief case. I spend a great deal of time in the car traveling to speaking engagements. A quick munch on a snack bar keeps the ol' tummy from growling while in front of an audience! (Keep a toothbrush handy, too, to keep the oats out of that winning smile!) Pudding makes a great snack when you have a sweet tooth. And now pudding is fat free and instant, which makes it easier to have around as a snack. My favorite recipe for pudding is to combine crushed pineapple and low-fat vanilla yogurt with pistachio pudding mix. Very tasty!

Perhaps my favorite snack of all time is popcorn. I eat popcorn all the time! I keep an air popper in my office and it is usually going all the time. Students know when I am in the office because they can smell popcorn all over the second floor of our building. I guess that I pop around 200 pounds of popcorn each year. And popcorn is a great snack to share. Students and other faculty come in to grab a handful of popcorn before going to class! To flavor my popcorn I use fat-free seasoning salt. Another idea is to flavor your air-popped popcorn with olive oil and basil to give it a unique taste.

As speakers, there are certain foods that we want to avoid prior to giving presentations. It is best NOT to consume chocolate, quantities of sugar, dairy products, or carbonated drinks in the few hours before you speak. These substances stimulate the glands in your mouth and throat, changing the moisture balance. We often know that there are other food-type items that also affect that moisture. You must realize what does and does not work for you. For most people, the moisture generated is a thick mucus.

## KEEPING YOUR MOUTH MOISTURIZED

What results when that heavy mucus is formed is the need to swallow, clear your throat, or drink more liquids. Each person really needs to determine through experience the kinds of food and drinks he or she can or cannot consume prior to speaking. The recovery times for eating such foods will vary with each individual. The time necessary for the body to recover could be as long as 24 hours. A large, rich chocolate and ice cream dessert can still be with you the next day. With other foods, the time could be as short as 15 minutes. You have to know how your body reacts to what you consume and for how long.

Drink plenty of water. The goal for most of us is eight glasses a day. The eight glasses rule is a general rule—some people require more; some require less. You can check with your doctor or monitor your urine color. Depending on the other supplements you may be taking, the goal is to have the color be clear. Try increasing your intake until you achieve the goal. This may seem like a lot or be quite difficult to accomplish in spite of the benefits it provides: healthier skin, ridding the body of impurities, and keeping the vocal folds moist. Maintaining a regular consumption of water will keep all the cells of your body adequately moisturized. When your body is under additional pressure to keep your vocal process moist, the necessary moisture will be available. Drinking water throughout the day did not come easily for me (especially when nature called and I was having to leave my office every half hour to relieve myself). But, believe it or not, your body becomes accustomed to the increased amounts of water and is able to accommodate it much more easily.

I have known some folks who do not like the taste of water. They prefer that the liquids they drink have some kind of taste, and I can't argue with that. But if you are one of those people, you may want to purchase a water filter to improve the taste. I have a portable water filter that I keep in my office that did not cost me very much. It vastly improves the taste of the water and removes chlorine and other chemicals, which I think makes the water better for you. Other

folks like to add lemon to their water to give it a little extra
flavor. And if you search your kitchen cabinets, you can probably find a plastic water bottle so you can keep a constant
supply of water with you.

Water is the primary way to keep your body and your vocal
mechanism adequately supplied with moisture. When you are
about to make a presentation, there are also additional ways to
keep your vocal folds moisturized. Gargling with salt water
solutions, drinking tea, or using cough drops work for some
folks. A product that I have relied on through the years is
Entertainer's Secret Throat Relief. It contains glycerin, aloe
vera, and water. A few sprays into your nose and throat gives
you a soothing feeling in your throat and nasal passages.
Entertainer's Secret can be found in most drug stores. If you are
unable to find it in stores, I invite you to contact me so that
you are able to obtain this great product.

Entertainer's Secret is great to have when you're on the
road speaking. A great deal of traveling also means changes in
climate, temperature, and humidity. For those of you who
have allergy difficulties, traveling through a heavily polli-
nated area can be devastating. Entertainer's Secret can help
relieve irritation in the nose and throat caused by allergic
reactions. For those of us who may have problems with dry,
sore throats in the mornings, dry mouth from airplane
flights, or after speaking for long periods of time, a few sprays
can revive your throat and eliminate any discomfort.

Another trick I've learned is to keep dried lemon in the
office with me or in my briefcase. I cut fresh lemon into small
pieces (the meat and the peel) and let them dry three or four
days. Once it is dried, it is easy to carry the lemon with you in
a plastic bag. Just pop the lemon in your mouth whenever it's
needed. The ascorbic acid that is released stimulates the glands
in your mouth and reduces the "dry mouth" sensation. This

also gives the throat and the vocal folds a little moisturizing. And it helps to battle not-so-fresh-smelling breath!

## EXERCISE: KEEP THAT BODY FIT

When anyone mentions staying fit and being healthy, we all know what comes next. Exercise! For some of us, the mere mention of the word strikes fear and dread in our hearts. Most speakers don't even want to do voice exercises like those mentioned in this book. Usually our intentions are good, but we just don't quite measure up to what fitness experts say we should do. We don't measure up to what we know we should do either. But no matter how much we don't want to accept it, a daily routine of aerobic exercise is one of the best things we can do for our bodies. It's hard to get started and even harder to maintain our routines, but the facts are . . . you just have to do it! Just do it.

Exercise gurus will tell you different stories about how often you should do your exercise routine, whether aerobic or weight training. Generally, this amounts to every other day or three days a week. Based on conversations with lots of speakers who do exercise, I recommend exercising every day, seven days a week. If I do that regular pattern, my body stays in shape. If I don't do that, I never reach that comfort level. You have to do what is right for your body.

I have chosen walking as the best exercise routine for me. For my spirit and my body, I began walking in the early mornings. I arise every morning at 5:00 A.M. This allows me a half hour to feed the dog, drink some water, meditate on scripture, and get dressed so that I'm on the street by 5:30. I have several set routes of three miles each. My goal is to make the complete loop through our residential area in 30 minutes. It took me quite a while to work up to the 10-minute mile, but I finally got there! Whatever you decide for yourself, whether it's walking or running, in the mornings or the evenings, exercise so that your heart is at a good aerobic level and is kept there long enough to strengthen your system.

Walking is usually the easiest form of exercise to engage in. It costs virtually nothing except time and requires very little equipment, just comfortable clothes, shoes, and socks. The best thing about walking is you can do it while you are on the road! Circle the hallways of your motel or the common areas of the local mall. And walking is usually a not-too-intimidating exercise routine that you can invite friends to do with you. Sometimes having a like-minded buddy (a spouse, friend, child, neighbor, or coworker) to exercise with can help to encourage you and keep you motivated. At conventions and meetings, some of the most fun moments I've had are those networking opportunities when walking each morning. Walk using good posture, not leaning forward. Raise your rib cage and keep it raised. Squeeze those abs and the muscles of your buttocks and swing your arms.

My own experience with keeping a daily routine has given me many advantages, both physical and mental. I lost weight, and that was fantastic. But even better than that was the self-esteem boost that losing the weight gave me. Doing my walking routine in the morning gives me energy to work longer days and to be more productive. Exercise as an activity has never been fun for me. Getting hot and sweaty with no immediate observable results to show for it has always been hard for me to justify. I always felt I had something more important to do. I never would have thought that I could keep the routine going over the years. I continue to look forward to my walks. It provides time alone to think, meditate, and prioritize my day. When I walk early in the mornings, the neighborhood is quiet and calm. I think of this as a time to indulge myself because most of the time, the rest of my day is never this free of distractions! One final note, it is a great time to pray.

## Trying to Stay with an Exercise/Daily Routine

As professional speakers, many of us stay very busy a great deal of the time. We travel, we go to conventions, we do seminars, but we still need to make time for our personal lives. Although we want to feel productive, we need to seek balance. The need for productivity should never overshadow the care our bodies deserve. We should never neglect good health in the name of productivity. Our bodies deserve a certain amount of attention and we need to make the time to fulfill that obligation. First and foremost, we need to get adequate sleep. (And don't forget that aerobic exercise can help you sleep better!) Most of us can't keep the schedules that we had as youngsters. We just can't pull "all nighters" to finish our work and meet deadlines. Withholding adequate sleep from our bodies only makes for unnecessary "wear and tear" and fatigue. In our commitment to maintaining healthy regimens, this includes a commitment to maintaining consistent body clock hours. The time we go to bed to sleep and when we arise are often dictated by the activities we are involved in. My recommendation is that you structure your activities, when it is possible, around your sleep schedule. If you want the best possible routine for your body, plan on going to sleep and arising at the same times, seven days a week.

How many of us know that our sleep-in schedule on weekends messes us up the first one or two days of the next week. The consistent sleep schedule works. There are times when we can't maintain the sleep schedule. Notice the reaction from your body. The sleep pattern you use impacts your productivity. Regular sleep helps. Believe me, your body will thank you for it!

As a whole, give thought to and do what you can to keep your voice and your body healthy. This means taking precautions in everyday situations. Minimize your exposure to dust, smoke, and noise. Dust and smoke can irritate the membranes of your nasal passages and your throat. These particles in the air can also lodge themselves in the small pockets in the membranes of your lungs, making the oxygen exchange more difficult. Long-term exposure to loud noise can cause early hearing loss. Avoid alcohol and recreational drugs. More than damaging your body, they can damage your spirit. But I do acknowledge that if you have diabetes, asthma, high blood pressure, clinical depression, etc., you can't avoid certain drugs necessary to maintain your general level of health.

One health-oriented routine that you must follow daily is frequent hand washing. After visits to the restroom, blowing your nose, coughing, sneezing, or using items other people have handled (office equipment, phones, doors, coffee pots, etc.) are good times to wash your hands. You will want to be especially mindful if you have "little ones" around. They have a tendency to catch germs at school and bring them home. Teaching them to wash their hands frequently will help to keep them (and you!) healthy.

It may seem simple and elementary, but take notice of how you wash your hands. When you lather up the soap, it is best to scrub your hands for at least 30 seconds. It's even a good idea to give your hands a second washing to ensure that they are clean. To keep your hands clean, use a paper towel to open the door when you are finished (particularly in public restrooms).

Cover your mouth and nose with a tissue when you sneeze or cough and then dispose of it. This may seem simple and it is something we learned as children, but some people don't do it. Also, be sure to keep your hands away from your face to reduce their exposure to germs. This routine of washing hands, using tissues, and keeping hands away from the face may sound familiar to you. It brings back memories of your mother or your doctor telling you to "cover your mouth" or "wash those hands," but it works. It will keep you healthier.

It is also important to follow the advice of health care professionals, especially before taking any medications. You may need to consult a doctor before starting your exercise regimen to receive a full physical exam. Don't end up hurting yourself while you thought you were helping yourself. This checkup will just ensure that you are in good health and your body will be physically able to begin exercising.

Each of us really needs to check with an otolaryngologist to allow that ear, nose, and throat physician the opportunity to get some benchmark data regarding our communication mechanisms. If they are familiar with us and our physical conditions, their resources are available to us when we are on the road and have a problem with our voices. They may be able to prescribe healthful solutions or the necessary medication to get us quickly back on the speaking trail.

Another good doctor to have on your side is a chiropractor. Too many of us have spinal alignment problems that won't go away. These problems only tend to get worse with time. My regular monthly visits keep me aligned and help me maintain good posture.

## SPIRITUAL ELEMENTS:
## MORE CRITICAL THAN WE REALIZE

Finally, and this could be the most important of all suggestions I share with you, keep a positive focus. And **SMILE**!!! Smiling releases healing endorphins; smiling makes you feel better. I would like to challenge you to keep a positive attitude.

It is very easy to become aggravated and frustrated when things don't go right at work or when someone upsets us. It is also very easy to let these happenings bring our spirits down and affect our work and our interactions with others. I hope that you won't allow that to happen in your daily lives. Always try to **smile,** encourage others, be enthusiastic, and use humor. Be the upbeat character in your office, in your household, and in your civic organization. People who stay positive usually feel better about themselves, about others, and about the work they do. Sometimes, it is difficult to be the upbeat character, but others will appreciate you for it. In the midst of people who are grumpy and appear downtrodden (they have their shoulders rolled forward and are slumping over), fellow workers will appreciate your character and nature. The upbeat character is usually hard to come by, so be an original!

Law enforcement personnel and the media are making a big deal out of road rage. Road rage appears to be our personal reaction to what other people do as they drive. In other circles, your reaction to what other people do is called stress. Since this book is about communication choices, let's talk about the biggest choice you can make. Decide not to let anything that anyone does make you angry. You can choose whether to be offended or not—it's your choice.

This challenge I am making to you reminds me of a saying that has stayed with me through the years. Quite a few years ago, I was visiting an old friend in her office. Above her desk was a poster that read: **IT'S HARD TO FLY LIKE AN EAGLE WHEN YOU'RE SURROUNDED BY TURKEYS!!!** This is very true. It is very hard sometimes to be the bright spot and the encourager, but your positive focus will be remembered by many folks.

# PRACTICE

# Perfect Practice
# Leads to the Best
# Performance

The need to practice our presentations should be obvious. We want to be sure we know what we are going to say. However, there is an element regarding the practice routine that we tend to forget. **All** the delivery elements need to be rehearsed, not just the sequencing of words. We may "know" the material. We may have memorized the words or maybe just the sequence of ideas and now we just plan to "wing" the rest of our delivery, such as pitch changes, volume, and the rest. However, playing the video back and watching the awkward or inappropriate movements and the not-so-pleasant sounds or awkward pauses should remind us that rehearsal could have fixed those delivery behaviors.

All aspects of delivery must be planned and rehearsed. So rehearse out loud, in costume, with all the speech materials available. Gestures, movement, voice changes, and even the handling of overheads need practice. We should even rehearse our responses to all the other things that could go wrong: losing lights due to power outages, an audience member collapsing with a medical emergency, the last overhead bulb expiring, a fire, the sprinkler system going off for no obvious reason, becoming physically ill and needing the restroom IMMEDIATELY—and the list goes on.

We each have some "favorite" overused gestures or vocal patterns that aren't truly communicating, at least, not as well as we thought they once did. We need to get ourselves actively involved in self-evaluation, especially before our presentations. Take the opportunity to use videotape. Watch the playback of the same presentation more than a couple of times. Most people will only see and attend to the surface or cosmetic issues during those first two or three viewings. Checking it out repeatedly will allow you to identify the subtle changes that could make the delivery better. At least subtle changes might make the delivery less distracting. However, there is a good chance that even with repeated viewing, the subtle stuff still won't seem obvious enough for us to expend the energy necessary to try to achieve a change. This is a good time to bring in the assistance of a colleague who understands delivery and is willing to be honest with you. Most professional speakers would improve their speech delivery and expand their business if they would hire a delivery coach. Those subtle delivery concerns as seen or heard on video, which are a part of your habit patterns, need the trained eyes and ears of a specialist.

When evaluating your video performance, notice behaviors that are distracting to you. These same behaviors might be viewed as distracting to your audience members. Were those behaviors related to your feelings of what you might term stage fright? Actually, we are not supposed to use that outdated set of words. It's now referred to as communication apprehension. Communication apprehension-related feelings are really common among all speakers. But the actual behaviors resulting from those feelings are rare, especially among professional speakers. Professional speakers have learned not to show their apprehension by exhibiting behaviors. If in fact you feel apprehension in speaking situations, it is part of your job not to give away those feelings to your audience. Speakers who tell their audiences that they are fearful or that their knees are shaking only set the audience up to look for those behaviors.

Contrary to popular belief, most of the apprehension in speaking comes from uncertainty regarding the content rather than the actual delivery variables. If we aren't as organized as we need to be, if we aren't as familiar with the material as we need to be, or if we aren't as confident in how we plan to deliver this presentation as we need to be, we may very well experience mental anxiety and exhibit distracting communication behaviors.

My first recommendation is to be prepared. Outline your presentation. Be very familiar with the content you plan to share. Practice all phases of the delivery until you are very comfortable with not just the words or sentences but also the movement, eye contact, use of visuals, etc. All of it needs to be rehearsed. Finally, as you rehearse and actually deliver the presentation, be aware of and use *The Big Three.*

## FINAL THOUGHTS: BUT IT ISN'T OVER YET

Often speakers are plagued with sounding like they are dialect-ridden. Dialect reduction can be a long-term project. As aware as you are now of all the vocal and movement variables, you should be able to recognize and reduce the distracting elements. But as mentioned before, you will need help. We simply don't attend to all the variables necessary to be able to initiate and sustain the change process successfully by ourselves. Choose your coach wisely. Contact me if you need help finding one. The ideal coaching relationship is face-to-face and one-on-one. But amazing results can be achieved through videotape and teleconferencing. You are the key. Are you willing to listen, learn, and make changes?

## POLITICALLY CORRECT: BE EXTRA CAREFUL

In our ever-changing cultural setting we have more and more frequent opportunities to do or say the inappropriate thing.

Unless we have thought through all those potential risk opportunities and changed our first-reaction verbal responses, we are very likely to say or do the wrong thing. The only advice I can give you is to constantly check the condition of your heart. If you find that you have fleeting moments when judgmental thoughts regarding individuals or groups of people cross your mind and often your lips, then deal with those thought patterns. Unless you do deal with and change those thought patterns and the resulting verbal behaviors, you are going to continue placing yourself in an at-risk position.

Our goal is to walk-our-talk. Our value to others and to our business opportunities is strongly related to what our audience is able to "read-between-the-lines." Audience members must have confidence in us as speakers in order to have confidence in our messages, and ultimately, to have confidence in themselves. If we harbor negative thoughts and feelings, we are less likely to get that confidence ball rolling and develop a positive relationship. If our hearts are in the right place, we don't have to hide what's in them. If we find ourselves watching what we say and do, so as not to reveal what is in our hearts, we are placing ourselves at risk in front of our audiences. We risk not only being politically incorrect, but we risk being seen as phony.

We must be aware of unguarded careless comments by checking what is in our hearts. It's a strange reality that most of us may not know or believe we have a problem. Often even our best friends won't tell us. Even if they did, we would not believe them. We are confident we can control what we say. Many of us can recall a situation where we were caught off-guard in front of an audience and we reacted verbally like we might have done in private. Those careless words or actions reveal the true condition of our hearts. The results can be devastating. We crush all possibilities of belief or confidence. My caution to you: Be aware of the true condition of your heart.

# A ppendix A

## VOCAL EXERCISES

Practice the Big Three: (1) good posture, (2) neck and shoulder muscle relaxation, and (3) breath support by taking cleansing breaths and lots of vocal exercises for two to five minutes every hour for every hour you are awake for the rest of your life.

1.  Good posture:
    a.  unlock knees
    b.  level pelvis
    c.  tuck tummy
    d.  raise rib cage
    e.  shoulders back and down
    f.  head up and back

    If you are holding your head erect and in proper position, there will be a straight line from the top of your ear to the top of your shoulder to the top of your hip bone to the center of your foot.

2.  Relaxed neck and shoulder muscles: Train yourself to relax these muscles and recognize when they are tense. Involuntary neck pulls are unattractive and send negative messages to you and to the rest of the world.

3.  Efficient breath support: Using good posture, take a cleansing breath. Inhale by expanding your lower thoracic/upper abdominal area, keeping your tummy

firm and your shoulders back, down, and relaxed. Then, keeping good posture, exhale quickly, forcing out the old air, completely emptying your expiratory reserve and increasing the oxygen exchange before you fill your lungs again. In order to get the feel of a cleansing breath, visualize your breathing apparatus being on your back below your rib cage.

Good posture, relaxed neck and shoulder muscles, and efficient breath support must be in place when exercising or when attempting to develop new voice quality, rate, pitch, or volume habits if those changes are to be sustained over time. If these habits are not maintained, the voice changes will be short-lived and not likely to develop into new habits.

1.  Trill/swallow
    a.  With good posture, relaxed neck and shoulders, and efficient breath support, initiate a cleansing breath.
    b.  Elevate your chin toward the ceiling.
    c.  Trill your tongue off the alveolar ridge, and
    d.  Hum, going up in pitch.
    e.  When you hit your highest pitch, swallow.
    f.  Keeping your chin elevated, restart the trill, coming down in pitch to your lowest pitch.
    g.  Do another cleansing breath.

    This exercise will strengthen the muscles that keep the vocal folds together during speech and help reduce excessive air loss while speaking.

2.  Ah–ng; denasal and nasal, soft palate push-ups.
    Hold your jaw open, with the tip of your tongue on your lower teeth, raising and lowering only the soft palate and the back of your tongue as you repeat the nasal and denasal sounds.

3.  Echo. Reduce breathiness by producing an echo off a wall to make vocal fold movement more efficient. This

is not a volume exercise. This exercise can also be done using the windshield of a car. If you don't hear an echo, you are being too breathy.

4. Lip muscles.
   a. Motor boat: Pull your lips loosely together, then blow through them, causing them to flap in the wind.
   b. Trumpet: Pull your lips tightly together, forcing air through the center of your lips. By adjusting the muscle tension of your lips, you can change the pitch of the tone produced.

These two exercises stimulate your lip muscles and their nerve endings, encouraging you, to move your lip muscles more when you speak.

   c. Pencil: Place a pencil in your mouth behind your canine teeth, place your tongue under the pencil and overexaggerate the lip movement to speak clearly.
   d. Lip over: Put your lower lip out, up, and over your upper lip; then put your upper lip out, down, and over your lower lip; repeat. This will stretch theupper and lower lip to encourage movement.

5. Hum at optimum pitch; then hum, slowly expanding the range up and down the scale. Do this exercise slowly. Take five minutes. Good for warming up your vocal folds before you attempt to speak or sing.

6. Place of resonation and voicing. p-b, t-d, and k-g.

Going from front to back and from back to front, a sound placement exercise.

7. Expanding the pharynx; drop the base of the tongue, and widen the cavity, as in a yawn. Use negative practice to hear and feel the differences between the sound produced when your throat is relaxed and the pharynx is enlarged and when the tongue is up and the throat is tight.

8. Cleansing breaths, with and without "arm-flys": Straighten arms, starting with the hands low and moving arms up and out to the sides, inhaling as you move. Increase the time taken to inhale (up to 60 seconds or more) while continuing to do rapid exhales. Exhale, blowing out all the air possible, then completely fill your lungs. This is a great exercise to be used as a stress reducer.

9. Standing push-up on a wall or through a doorway: Say an "ah" until you are as close to the wall as you can get, then stop the "ah" and close the vocal folds. Notice the diminishing breathiness as you approach the wall.

10. Standing pelvic thrusts: To strengthen the lower back and abdominal muscles, to help support your good posture.

11. Obliques Crunch: Lie down with your lower back pressed to the floor, your knees bent, and your right ankle on your left knee. Place your hands under your head, keeping your elbows wide apart. Then lift your left shoulder a few inches, keeping your right shoulder on the floor. Lead with your shoulder, not your elbow. Hold for a beat, then return your shoulder to the floor. Avoid pulling your neck forward. Do four sets of 20 crunches—two sets on each side.

12. Obliques Stretch: Still lying on the floor, draw your legs up to your chest, bend your knees, and relax—there is no need to pull your knees closer than is comfortable. Then rotate your arms slowly to the right and your legs and head to the left. Hold for 30 seconds, and repeat on the other side.

13. Bicycles: Again on your back, raise your knees so that your thighs are perpendicular to the floor and your calves are parallel to the floor. Raise your upper back off the floor, keeping your neck straight, and with your hands behind your head twist your upper body from side to side. As you twist pull one knee toward the opposite shoulder. For instance, if you twist to the left

then pull your left knee in towards your right elbow and extend the other leg (your leg does not have to be completely straight) without letting it touch the floor.

14. Extensions: While lying flat on the floor, extend legs so that your knees are partially bent. Raise your feet upward. Use the same motion as a crunch and reach towards your feet with your arms extended. In doing this, keep your neck straight and bring your upper back off the floor.

Note: During crunches, extensions, and oblique stretches, exhale on the way up—blowing out through your mouth—and inhale on the way down—through the nose. During bicycles, alternate breathing on twists.

15. Posture "off the wall": Buns, shoulders, and head should all leave the wall at the same time.

16. Broom handle, in the I-give-up position, with the handle in front of the wrists and in back of the shoulders, to help align the shoulders back and down.

17. Yardstick, under your belt in back, hold your head back to the yardstick, notice how often your head is "turtled" forward when you reach for items.

18. Hands-over-head: Arms straight, on your back, with a book or small weights in each hand, exhale as you make the arch from over-your-head to next-to-your-sides while keeping your back straight and against the floor. Inhale, expanding your rib cage, returning your straight arms to over your head. As you keep your shoulders flat to the floor, you strengthen your shoulder and rib cage muscles.

19. Lower back reach: While seated, hands behind your head, bend forward between your legs attempting to touch your elbows to the floor. Hold the position as your back muscles relax and as long as the stretch can continue.

20. Head raise stretches: Lie on the floor, face down, nose and forehead touching the floor, with your tummy off

the floor (back straight). With each stretch, keeping
your nose and forehead parallel to the floor, lift your
head straight up off the floor.

> *Stretch 1:* With arms stretched flat on the floor above
> your head, moving only your head and neck, lift
> your head.
>
> *Stretch 2:* With fists tucked under your shoulders, lift
> head straight up off the floor.
>
> *Stretch 3:* With arms behind your back, lift head
> straight up off the floor.

For all three stretches, start with 5 repetitions and work
up to 50.

21. Leg raise stretches: Lie on the floor face down with nose
    and forehead touching the floor. Keep your tummy off
    the floor, using the backs of your hands against your
    cheekbones to hold your head straight. Keeping the legs
    straight, lift one leg off the floor at a time. Alternate
    right and left leg. Start with 5 repetitions of each and
    work up to 50.

22. Lower back rotation: Lie on the floor on your back,
    hands out on each side in the hands-up position, calves
    placed on the seat of a chair, pushing the small of your
    back to the floor. Raise your pelvis in a pelvic thrust
    using your lower back and abdominal muscles rather
    than pushing your heels into the chair seat. Start with 5
    repetitions and work up to 50.

23. Lower back stretch: Sitting on your feet and knees, bend
    forward from your hips till your nose and forehead
    touch the floor with your arms straight out above your
    head on the floor. Hold the stretch for several minutes.

24. Neck and shoulder isometric: Making sure the posture is
    correct, bend one arm across your chest and grasp that
    elbow with the other hand. Turn your head over the
    shoulder of the pulled elbow, pushing it in that direc-
    tion as you tighten your neck muscles. Hold that posi-
    tion for at least five seconds. Relax the muscles of your

neck, then slowly turn your head to the front, then to the other side and push your head in the other direction, tightening your neck muscles. Do this sequence with each elbow several times, especially when you experience neck tension.

25. Cardiovascular: Walking, aerobic walking, jogging, swimming, running, bicycling, etc. Any activity done on a daily basis continuously for over 20 minutes which will get your heart working will help keep you healthy and active.

26. Dry cough: Do a cough without vocalizing, expelling lots of air while doing so.

27. Whatever exercises will help you relax, stretch and strengthen your lower back and abdominal muscles, your upper torso, and your neck and shoulders muscles (regardless of the quality of your physical condition) should be done on a daily basis.

# Appendix B

## VOWEL CHART
### indicating the position of the hump in the tongue for the production of each sound

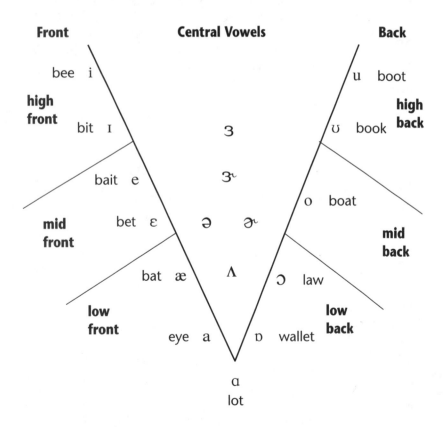

# About Toastmasters International

If the thought of public speaking is enough to stop you dead in your tracks, it may have the same effect on your career.

While surveys report that public speaking is one of people's most dreaded fears, the fact remains that the inability to effectively deliver a clear thought in front of others can spell doom for professional progress. The person with strong communication skills has a clear advantage over tongue-tied colleagues—especially in a competitive job market.

Toastmasters International, a nonprofit educational organization, helps people conquer their pre-speech jitters. From one club started in Santa Ana, California, in 1924, the organization now has more than 170,000 members in 8,300 clubs in 62 countries.

## How Does It Work?

A Toastmasters club is a "learn by doing" workshop in which men and women hone their communication and leadership skills in a friendly, supportive atmosphere. A typical club has 20 members who meet weekly or biweekly to practice public speaking techniques. Members, who pay approximately $35 in dues twice a year, learn by progressing through a series of 10 speaking assignments and being evaluated on their performance by their fellow club members. When finished with the basic speech manual, members can select from among 14 advanced programs that are geared toward specific career needs. Members also have the opportunity to develop and practice leadership skills by working in the High Performance Leadership Program.

Besides taking turns to deliver prepared speeches and evaluate those of other members, Toastmasters give impromptu talks on assigned topics, usually related to current events. They also develop listening skills, conduct meetings, learn parliamentary procedure and gain leadership experience by serving as club officers. But most importantly, they develop self-confidence from accomplishing what many once thought impossible.

The benefits of Toastmasters' proven and simple learning formula has not been lost on the thousands of corporations that sponsor in-house Toastmasters clubs as cost-efficient means of satisfying their employees' needs for communication training. Toastmasters clubs can be found in the U.S. Senate and the House of Representatives, as well as in a variety of community organizations, prisons, universities, hospitals, military bases, and churches.

## How to Get Started

Most cities in North America have several Toastmasters clubs that meet at different times and locations during the week. If you are interested in forming or joining a club, call (714) 858-8255. For a listing of local clubs, call (800) WE-SPEAK, or write Toastmasters International, PO Box 9052, Mission Viejo, California 92690, USA. You can also visit our website at http://www.toastmasters.org.

As the leading organization devoted to teaching public speaking skills, we are devoted to helping you become more effective in your career and daily life.

Terrence J. McCann
*Executive Director, Toastmasters International*

# Allyn & Bacon Order Form
## The Essence of Public Speaking series